King of Fashi

King of Fashion
The Autobiography
of Paul Poiret

Translated by Stephen Haden Guest

V&A Publishing

First published by J. B. Lippincott Company, 1931
This edition published by V&A Publishing, 2009
V&A Publishing
Victoria and Albert Museum
South Kensington
London SW7 2RL

Distributed in North America by
Harry N. Abrams, Inc., New York

ISBN 978 1 85177 564 4
Library of Congress Control Number 2008937534
10 9 8 7 6 5 4 3 2 1
2013 2012 2011 2010 2009

Cover design by V&A Design

Printed in Great Britain by CPI Bookmarque

V&A Publishing
Victoria and Albert Museum
South Kensington
London SW7 2RL
www.vam.ac.uk

To the memory of my mother

Contents

I
Youth

I am a Parisian of Paris. I was born in its heart, in the Rue des Deux-Ecus, in the First Arrondissement, where my father was set up as a cloth merchant at the sign of Good Hope. It was a little, narrow street which joined the Rue du Louvre and the Rue Berger.

My father's shop occupied the whole frontage on the street level. Opposite, there were petty traders whose children swarmed in the street, there was the fruiterer's wife, always with a perfectly finished *coiffure*, the Alsatian shoemaker, Liebengut, Fréchinier the carpenter, Michaud the wine merchant, and Badier the butcher, now a millionaire. A little further was the manufactory of *marrons glacés* and compotes which, at certain times, perfumed the whole little quarter and filled me with delight.

I am told that one of the first words I uttered was: 'Cron papizi,' and the initiate understood that this was my way of asking for a pencil and paper (*crayon et papier*). Thus, my vocation as a painter revealed itself before my vocation as a dressmaker; but my earliest works were not preserved – they seem to have had no interest or meaning save for myself.

My life passed between my mother's apartment on the first floor and my father's shop, whither I was sometimes allowed to go down. I had friends in the house: the cat, the dog, and an old servant, Edmond, who used his ingenuity to make primitive toys for me; with four bits of wood he could make either a chariot or a billiard table, and he encouraged my anti-social instincts by teaching me to bombard with pins the employees of the Louvre, debonair wayfarers bearing on their shoulders a light cargo of inflated balloons, that burst beneath my fire.

I often went for walks with my mother, and it gave me great pleasure to accompany her into the shops, whose mingled smell of dust and perfume I loved; but above all when she went visiting: then it was my delight to listen to the chat and commonplaces of the ladies, while giving the impression that I was quite busy playing at something else.

1

I was always very well dressed: I remember a costume of black velvet I was very proud of, and I had a little gold ring encrusted with turquoise flowers. One day, as we were going to the bazar at the Town Hall, I put it down, as I passed by, on a table on the pavement outside a café. An hour later we returned the same way, and I was very surprised not to see my ring there in the place where I had left it. I uttered an exclamation, my mother asked me what was the matter, and I explained to her my disillusionment. She deplored my *naïveté*, and told me that I must always be on guard against thieves. Already at that time I had a confidence in others that has handicapped me all my life. I did not believe in thieves: but I begin to believe in them, to-day.

I remember that I had very little appetite, and there were innumerable scenes to make me swallow a few mouthfuls of meat. One day my father had promised me that, if I would eat a beefsteak, he would give me a Punchinello. I had seen one that pleased me because of its colours in the window of the 'Paradis des Enfants,' which was a shop in our neighbourhood, and scarcely was the last mouthful in my mouth before I rushed to seek my Punchinello, which I brought back triumphantly.

My father was kind, but he was ashamed of his feelings, and in appearance he was dry and crusty. My mother was charming, full of gentle sweetness, and of an education and knowledge very much above her station.

I remember watching the growth of their prosperity, and I saw the joy they took in enriching and embellishing their home. They bought, in the successive exhibitions of 1878, 1889, and 1900, everything that was our patrimony. It was not always very suitable, but it marked an aspiration towards the best, a progression towards the beautiful. Culture cannot be improvised.

A simple story will show you better than a long preamble to what social class I belonged. My paternal grandmother had nineteen brothers and sisters, all living. They constantly met together on holidays, at the houses of the more prosperous amongst them; most of them belonged to the small bourgeoisie, and lived in the Issy-Les-Moulineaux district.

One day, when I was seven years old (and I remember it as if it were yesterday), I was told that my Aunt Paul was dying and that I must go to see her for the last time. I was taken to Uncle Paul's house and he greeted me, saying: 'Bichette is ill, you must not make a noise,' and he accompanied me into his wife's room. I did not see her, so high-perched was she upon a raised bed, but I picked out a red eiderdown, and a crocheted lace coverlet, and, amidst massed pillows, a large, pointed, very pale nose. I was held under my arms and lifted up so that I could reach her and embrace her. She spoke to me a few poisoned words in which there was something about heaven, and I was put down again on the floor.

In the corridor I found Uncle Paul, at a loose end, marching up and down in his slippers, going continually from the parrakeet to the grandfather clock. He was getting old, and sometimes lost contact with reality.

A few days later the funeral took place. At the stated hour, in the Boulevard du Lycée at Issy, the twenty brothers and sisters with their wives and husbands were there in frock coats and top hats, or with black mourning shawls, aligned along the pavement. We went to the church where, naturally, Uncle Paul occupied the first chair in the first row. I was behind him. He was nervy, and seemed to be looking for someone. He turned round anxiously, and gazed at the uncles and aunts whom he saw arriving and taking their places, and suddenly, turning towards his neighbour, he said to him: 'Well, what about the old lady, where is she, Bichette?' His neighbour was Uncle Denis, a gilder by profession, who ought to have been accustomed to the need for discretion. He did not gild the pill for him, and with a gesture of both his hands he pointed out the catafalque, saying: 'Well, there you are.' Then Uncle Paul realised why he was there, and burst into tears like a child.

When we left the church we walked in procession behind the hearse and my neighbour, an old man in a frock coat, turned to me and asked me what I was called and who I was: I said to him, 'It is I, Paul Poiret.' – 'But then you are Auguste's lad?' And calling all the others in witness, he said to them: 'Look here, this is Auguste's lad!'

My father had been petted by all these old greybeards, and I profited from his popularity and fame amongst them. Uncle Denis, the gilder, came up to me, and, showing me the cock on the church belfry, said to me: 'Do you see, it is I who gilded it and, you know, it wasn't warm up there.'

*

Our country house was situated quite near there, in the immediate neighbourhood of Paris, at Billancourt. It was a great square building with an immense park, that has since become the property of the Renault works, for the Renault family also came from Billancourt. The Renault boys never showed themselves to those who went to visit their parents; it was known that they amused themselves in an amateur workshop, amongst machinery, coupling rods and pistons, constructing their first motor, and if by chance one caught sight of them, they were covered with oil and grease; dishevelled slaves of their ideal, untamed captives of an idea.

It was at Billancourt that I saw the first automobile carriages do their first trials. Passers-by judged these engines harshly, and used to say: 'They are possibly very convenient, but they are not graceful: something is missing in front.' To these unimaginative citizens it was the horse that seemed to be missing. If it had not been for their prejudice, the engine would, perhaps, and more logically, have been placed at the rear.

I remember the years I passed at Billancourt, in the activity and the *dolce far niente* of childhood, when one is perpetually busy, although one never does anything. Boredom is unknown. The games that appealed to me most were not those of the children of my age. I created marvellous constructions and fountains, which I made to work by putting a barrel full of water in an overhanging tree; or else, inspired by the brilliance of the flowers, the geraniums and begonias that abounded in the flower borders of my grandmother along the lawns and terraces, I tried to make inks and colours by pressing their petals, but according to such primitive processes that, naturally, I never succeeded in achieving more than the irremediable staining of my face, my hands and my clothes. Or else I wanted to extract their perfume from the roses, and I confined them in bottles of alcohol or soda water, having at that age no notion of chemistry; or else I crushed them into hermetic boxes. Then one day I made a hole in one of the boxes and a horrible, musty odour escaped. I was very disillusioned, but never discouraged.

Above all, I organised fêtes, rejoicings to which I invited my family, and where there were buffets at which I offered a champagne of my own manufacture, a frightful mixture of lemons, white wine, and seltzer water. I picked up all the old iron in the vegetable garden and the orchard, I labelled it like a keeper, and I formed a museum of antiquities.

I do not recount all this in order to boast of my choice of pleasures, but because it may seem curious to see me already at that epoch interested in the things which later were to become the objects of my researches and my passions.

One evening I left Billancourt with my parents to go to the opening of the Exhibition of 1889. My father had special tickets. I was drunk with joy. Riding on my father's shoulders, I looked on at the fairy revelations of the luminous fountain, and I was as incapable of tearing my eyes from it, as to-day I am of forgetting its memory. I have often asked myself whether my taste for colour was not born on that night, amidst the phantasmagoria of pinks, greens, and violets.

I will not attempt to depict the enthusiasm of the multitude who saw this prodigy for the first time. When all the jets of water melted into a greenish opaline light, a voice was heard in the crowd crying in the silence: 'Ah! What fine Pernod!' and there was an explosion of very French laughter.

The Exhibition revealed to me other unforeseen wonders: the applications of electricity, the gramophone, etc. I wanted to know Edison, or to write to him to thank him and personally congratulate him on what he was giving to humanity. The Decauville Railway, the moving platform, the Marinoni machines, the mills for the manufacture of paper, for wool spinning, the brocades of Lyons – it seemed to me that all the secrets of life had revealed themselves to me simultaneously, and satisfied all my curiosities.

What lovely days!

Then the whole family went on a trip to Brittany, which might have made me lose for ever all taste for travelling, so bored was I. We made all our excursions in uncovered carriages, in landaus or victorias drawn by two horses. My mother and my sister took their ease on the padded seat, the gentlemen – my father and myself – occupied the little flap seat. Generally it was narrow and hard, and during the whole trip I would see nothing but my mother and my sister with their opened parasols, and I scarcely perceived the landscape save when we stopped in front of some shrine. Or else, sometimes I was beside the driver, and I inhaled the dust, and the stench of the horses. Fortunately, there were interminable hills, and we got out and walked on foot to lighten the weight. I gathered flowers along the slopes and made bouquets for my mother. The Celtic soul had not yet revealed itself to me, and kept all its mystery.

When I was twelve we left the sordid Rue des Deux-Ecus for the Rue des Halles. I went to the *Ecole Massillon*, where I met children of higher social origin than my own, and sometimes I was made to suffer by the comparison, as notably when I wore beige pantaloons which had been cut from some stuff probably left on account by my father's clients. When it rained the colour changed and became pinky mauve, which made all my delighted playmates point their fingers at me. I ought to have laughed, but I wept.

I had three sisters. They had scarlet fever one after the other. I was sent as a boarder to the school, to avoid infection. As I was very sensitive and affectionate I suffered a great deal at this separation from my family, for no other setting seemed to me as desirable as my home. What miserable evenings I spent in the dormitory of the school – it was so bare and had so little reassurance – listening to the bugle calls in the barracks of the Republican Guard, which were just opposite. I remained awake a long time after Lights Out, and then I would dream . . .

Did I already dream of stuffs and chiffons? I think I must have. Women and their toilettes drew me passionately; I went through catalogues and magazines burning for everything appertaining to fashion; I was very much of a dandy, and if I sometimes forgot to wash, I never forgot to change my collar.

I was only a middling pupil, and I took more interest in literature than mathematics. With a very good memory, retaining everything that pleased me and indifferent to everything else, it was possible for me to be the first of my class in one subject and the last in another; which surprised nobody. My schoolfellows liked me for my whimsical spirit, for my notebook was always covered with comic drawings, and they were competed for like the masterpieces of some great library.

At all the prize-givings I compensated my parents for their bitter disillusionment at my not winning prizes by successes of another sort; I could act a comedy and speak a monologue with a great deal of

daring and drollery. I soon won a reputation for this sort of entertainment, and I was invited everywhere for it.

My boyhood passed, divided between my studies, visits to my friends,
and my love of the theatre – where I spent nearly all my evenings.
Precisely at 7 o'clock my family sat down to dinner, and three-quarters
of an hour afterwards I was already at the Comédie Française, waiting
for the doors to open. Then I rushed along the stairs, taking them four
at a time, and installed myself in the best seat of the cheapest part,
which was called the amphitheatre, and cost one franc. It was Paradise.
It was there that I tasted my first literary delights, and there that I heard
all the classics. It was there I received my dramatic education beneath
the gleams of the great chandelier and the ceiling that was so close to
my head. Ah! the splendid hours I passed with Mounet-Sully, Got,
Bartet, de Feraudy, Réjane, Granier, Sarah Bernhardt, Guitry!

I have often wondered how the young people of to-day can do
without these delights and joys of the mind. I shall always see Mounet-
Sully in *Oedipus Rex*, blind, coming down the steps of the temple, and
saying in a suave voice:

'Children of ancient Cadmus, young successors . . .'

And Got, polishing his glasses in *L'Ami Fritz*, to put himself in
countenance, and veil his visible emotion.

And de Feraudy, in *Le Fils de Giboyer*, letting his pipe fall on the
carpet of the great salon:

'I will never take you out again.'

And Bartet in *Antigone*, wearing a robe of the purest, chastest
muslin, whose lower folds seemed shadowed by a curious effect of the
footlights.

And Réjane in *Ma Cousine*, with the little check tailormade she
changed before the eyes of the audience.

And Granier in *Amants*, weeping in the nocturnal blackness of the
Lake of Lugano.

And Sarah Bernhardt in *Gismonda, Princesse d'Orient*.

And de Max, a bishop of the first days of the Church, his little
bonnet of coral velvet lined with ermine.

Ah! The theatre of Sardou, of Lavedan, of Brieux, of Capus, of
Flers and Caillaret, of Maurice Donnay: by what has it all been
replaced?

I remember the fine subscription evenings at the *Gymnase* and the

Vaudeville, when all the bourgeoisie and all the financial powers that were listened to *Viveurs*, or *Nos Bons Villageois* or *Amants*. The women kept on their hats then, they were little bonnets with or without strings and plaited with velvet flowers, Parma violets or geraniums. Then, the *parterre* really was a flower garden. And furthermore, there were leg of mutton sleeves that did not match, and were cut from another stuff than the dress itself, and in the foyer, during the intervals, the rustling skirts that swept the waxed parquet with their ruches and their bouillonnés, which were also called sweepers. And then, I saw the bustles; and I can say, with François Coppée:

'. . . I did not find that so ridiculous.'

For cannot women wear anything and everything and do they not possess the secret of making beautiful and acceptable the most improbable and audacious things? These ornaments, that were called strapontines, were covered with massed stuffs, draped and worked and folded with art by the great makers of that day, and they seemed light, despite their profusion. And then, one discovered beneath this great pile a foot so tiny, so well curved into the russet kid, that its charm was irresistible. I have seen hats caracolling at the summits of high-dressed hair, light as butterflies, despite the weight of their decorations, so skilled are those artists who devote themselves to the embellishment of women.

At that time there took place, several times a year, great functions in which all the trends of fashion were revealed. I followed them passionately; they were the private-view days of picture-exhibitions, which to-day have fallen almost into desuetude. There one met not only all the young painters, armed with ladders and varnishing pots, but their models and their admirers and their clients, and there reigned throughout their whole world a special sort of snobbism, and a conscious striving for effect, which were the very parents of fashion. I went constantly to the exhibitions of painting, and I sought to discover in them those who were going to be the masters of the day after to-morrow. Clairin and Bouguereau seemed to me finished, Carolus Duran antiquated, and Bonnat heavy footed; my opinions were thought subversive, and terrified my family because of their independence. I lauded the painting of Cottet, then a beginner, and I liked the Impressionists.

I met artists every evening on the boat that took me to Billancourt, and I consolidated my beliefs as I listened to their talk. There was, notably, Rodin, a little thickset god, with flowing beard, who used to take the boat to go home to his house at Meudon. It took an hour to go from Pont-Royal to our destination; it was a tranquil space, this hour passed on the modest vessel after the fever of the day in Paris. The Auteuil Viaduct, the hillsides of Meudon and the sunsets behind the Observatoire, – they all compose in my memory a restful and assuaging harmony.

My father had a little canoe which he called *The Microbe*. We often went for trips on the water, or for fishing. One day he took me with M. Maurou, who was a great engraver of those days, and we had the surprise of hearing, in a little restaurant where we had stopped, a dishwasher singing at her work with the most marvellous notes; the emotion I felt is still vivid within me. M. Maurou returned several times to listen to her. He persuaded her that she ought to work at her voice, found a master for her, and made her enter at the Conservatoire. She became 'La Grande Delna,' who sang, and every-one knows how, *L'Attaque du Moulin, Falstaff,* and many other famous works.

In the years when the great Exhibition of '89 was being prepared, we saw, every morning and evening, the progress in the constructing of the Eiffel Tower, and each of us in the boat had his comment to make.

It was hard work for me to complete my work at school, for I was solicited by divers distractions, and by an impatience to taste all the joys of life. At eighteen I matriculated and my father, terrified lest I should choose a career for myself, sent me to one of his friends who was an umbrella manufacturer, to make me learn business there. It was a hard trial for me.

I cannot recall without sadness the melancholy house of this umbrella manufacturer, who was stupidity itself; I passed mortal days with him, cleaning and carrying pieces of dark silk.

My father had said to him:

'Listen, he is a boy who has a well developed *amour propre*. He might easily become over-proud; we must break him of that, I want him to learn everything from the beginning.'

So I was made to learn how to sweep, and my employer took a malign pleasure in seeing this educated young man, of whom he was secretly jealous, clothed in a blouse and armed with a broom. The lowest tasks were reserved for me, like that of stopping up the umbrellas. I am sure you don't know what that is. I will tell you: When an umbrella is finished there are in the silk, if it is not of irreproachable quality, little holes, due to imperfections in the weaving: I spent my time in opening the umbrellas and, with the help of a brush dipped into blackish gum, I stopped up these orifices.

Naturally, I thought only of how to escape from this occupation. I was given my chance when I was sent to the Bon Marché, to the Louvre, to the Trois-Quartiers, to deliver umbrellas. I crossed Paris in my blouse, a heavy bundle of umbrellas on my shoulder. The point of this breaking-in will not escape you, they wanted to smash my pride. One must concede that the method was not infallible, for my pride is still whole to-day.

I hated and despised a master who understood so little what use he might have made of my powers and my goodwill. My eyes filled with tears as I watched him write his letters, full of spelling mistakes, and I thought only of deceiving him and escaping from his power. I filched bits of silk that fell when the umbrellas were being cut, and I built up for myself a little treasury of remnants, which illuminated my dreams and stimulated my desires.

When I was back at home in the evening I withdrew into my room and imagined sumptuous toilettes, faëry panoplies. My sisters had presented me with a little wooden mannequin 40 centimetres high, and on this little model I pinned my silks and muslins. What delightful evenings I owed to this doll, whom I made successively a piquante Parisienne and an Eastern Queen.

And then I designed fantastical ensembles. My sketches were summaries, they were notations in Indian ink, and I remember that the idea was always clearly indicated, and that there was always some inventive detail, and some interesting special point.

One day, encouraged by a daring friend, I took some designs to Mme Chéruit, who was in the Maison Raudnitz Sœurs. I was successful, Mme Chéruit wanted to make my acquaintance immediately, and had me brought into her office from the dark passage where I was awaiting her opinion.

I had never seen anything more disturbing than this lovely woman in the midst of so much elegance. She was such as she has been drawn and described by the burin of the engraver Helleu. She was modelled in a dress of deep blue with a very high collar that took the shape of her chin, and was prolonged to the ears. From this sheath there rose a narrow white ruche in which was set her face. The fastening of her dress was invisible. Her hair, twisted up behind her head, formed, over her brow, a wave so cunningly disposed that all the periwinkle darts of her gaze were shadowed by it. I don't think that Mme Chéruit ever knew the captivating impression she made on this young whipper-snapper who was offering her his work, that was probably unworthy of her: but she made much of it and bought my little sketches, paid me 20 francs apiece, and engaged me to come back again. There were twelve drawings. It was a gold mine. Henceforth, I could avoid crossing Paris with my umbrellas on my back, and if I were still sent to make deliveries, I would make them in a cab. I felt born within me a taste for independence and freedom.

I formed the habit of visiting the great dressmaking houses, such as Doucet, Worth, Rouff, Paquin, Redfern. I always had difficulty in getting past the doorkeeper, because naturally I had not the right password for the underlings. They saw at once that I was not an habitué, but as soon as I was known I was welcomed everywhere. I felt consideration and interest awakening in my clients.

One day (it was in 1896), M. Doucet proposed to me that instead of laying my eggs in every basket, I should produce for him alone. He offered to keep me with him and to buy all my designs. When I told this to my father he refused to believe me, so little knowledge had he of my vocation, and so little confidence in my success. He wanted to accompany me to M. Doucet, in order to conform to the tradition that then insisted that one should be presented by one's parents. I still see myself with him, crossing the threshold of M. Doucet's most distinguished residence in the Rue de la Ville-L'Evêque, and I remember the impression of magnificence produced on me by my future master.

He was the perfection of handsomeness and elegance, exceedingly *soigné*, and looking as if he had just come out of a bandbox. His silky beard was already white, although he was then only forty-five. He was wearing a grey suit whose cloth was marked out in little concentric lozenges, and his white gaiters partially covered shoes that were so highly polished that I had never seen anything like them. I learned afterwards that this polish was obtained by a special process, and that his shoes had to be sent back to the factory to be repolished every time he wore them.

M. Doucet's whole setting was composed of engravings and pictures of the eighteenth century, and of rare and ancient furniture, but everything very restrained, and chosen with perfectly controlled taste. The velvet of the curtains and armchairs was moss green or mauve, and of precious quality. As I listened to him I thought that he was saying everything that I wanted to say, and that he was the man whom I wished to become. In my imagination, I was already the Doucet of the future. I did not want any other model in life save him. I would have liked to be able to have made myself in his image.

He said to my father that he had noticed in the Tuileries Dog Show a griffon exhibited under the name of Poiret. It was, in fact, my father's dog. My father offered it to him in exchange for the service he was doing me by taking me into his business. Then we withdrew, much moved by this cordial interview, and I, for my part, profoundly impressed by the majestic and affable features of this true *grand seigneur*.

It was at about this time that I had occasion to lunch with the famous director of the *Grands Magasins du Louvre*, M. Chauchard.

I knew M. Roy, the great horse-dealer, who was the purveyor of the Louvre's cavalry, the pride of the horsemanship contests of that time, – whose laurels have to-day been taken unto himself by Félix Potin. M. Roy invited me to lunch with M. Chauchard. Later I perceived that he wanted to avoid the horrors of a *tête-à-tête*, for M. Chauchard was the most artificial personage imaginable. All his riches could scarcely hide his essential poverty. On that particular day he certainly shone rather by his appetite than by his conversation. He ate in decorative fashion, methodically plunging his fork between two pompous white mustachios, that seemed like a military escort to his face. He was the very Emperor of the Philistines.

We lunched at the Hôtel Terminus, and the choice of restaurant seemed odd to me. When we were alone together, I asked M. Roy why he had thought it good to convoke us to this solemn and outmoded establishment. He explained that the Hôtel Terminus belonged to M. Chauchard, and that he rejoiced continually not only over the actual delights of the Château-Laffitte and Romanée, that made the reputation of his cellars, but also at the thought that each mouthful was bringing him in a profit. This preoccupation was ever with him, and his inner ear heard the hard cash falling into his pockets each time he chewed an ortolan.

I relate this as a characteristic of a vanished age, for I cannot believe that to-day there is anyone of such sort alive.

II
Chez Doucet

Thus I entered into this new life, this dressmaking where I was to meet with such success, and also with such tribulations. The Maison Doucet was then at the height of its prosperity. Before its doors in the Rue de la Paix one saw every day three lines of carriages, on which the coachbuilders of that epoch had lavished their invention. I shall always see in my memory the beautiful Comtesse de la Riboisière getting into her victoria on a fine, sunny day in November, and seating herself gracefully amidst the pale cloth cushions, while a footman wrapped a fur rug round her legs. What bearing! And how can I find words to describe General Robineau, the elegant sportsman who, in his tall hat and jacket, toured the Champs Elysées, whenever the weather was pleasant, on his tricycle?

It was a blessed time, when the cares and worries of life, the vexations of tax collectors and the threats of the Socialists had not yet crushed out the pleasures of thought and all joie de vivre. Women could go about the streets in all their elegance without becoming the butt of insults from navvies. The familiarity that reigned between the people and the great of the earth was charming. The great gentlemen who frequented the Rue de la Paix responded to the smiles of the midinettes. A pleasant camaraderie flowered all about.

Chez Doucet I remember delightful hours, and unforgettable people. I found myself very much at a loss when I was presented to the Old Guard, the Saleswomen. They were for the most part aged harpies installed in the house like mites in a cheese. They had a great ascendancy over their clientèle, spoke familiarly to the great ladies, and taking them by the waist would give them advice in parental tones; over all the personnel of the house they exercised an intolerable despotism. I absolutely must tell you of poor old Mother Tilliez, who had a Liberty satin robe of episcopal violet, and who, despite her seventy years, always dressed like a girl. She exerted herself to thwart me, as if I had given her some cause for offence. I think she must have hated my youth and independence. This strange personality,

14

ravaged by age and avarice, perished by suicide. She had a young lover with whom she was quarrelling one day, and, as he was threatening to leave the house, she said to him: 'If you do go, I shall be outside before you.' While he was going down the stairs, she threw herself from the window. Thus he found her on the pavement as he came out of the door.

I recall also the mask-face of Gorgone de Flavie, with the mahogany hair, and eyes that darted flaming hate; and also the honied Mlle Sannois, silver-haired, dressed in lace, with an inclined confidential air (I think some infirmity must have prevented her from holding her head erect) – her sweetness was no less dangerous.

I don't think I shall ever forget Eliane, who looked like some aged wild beast with multi-coloured mane. This feline wore on her head a pile of corkscrews that looked like a dyer's sample card. Her hair ranged from scarlet to Empire green, passing through all the tints of tobacco juice, oxtail, and onion peel. She reminded one of the swabs sailors use for washing down the deck, but a swab with a vine stem for its handle, so nervous, sinewy and inter-twisted was her neck. Two green lanterns, for her eyes, and the lipless mouth of a viper; such was the frightful visage of this wreck: she terrified me. I thought her a dangerous witch, an evil fairy. I imagined she had some mysterious and tragic life, but I was wrong, for Eliane lived with a hairdresser's assistant who, perhaps, had been so imprudent as to experiment on her with some new dyeing process.

While I sought by every means to make my importance felt in the House (for I was the head of the tailor department, and I had to keep a tight hand over the technical staff, who had much greater experience than I), Mesdames the Saleswomen worked to humiliate me before subordinates, and took a malicious pleasure in playing me tricks. Fortunately I had a few friends among the young ones: Mme Ventadour who was fair and very pretty, Mme Lemesmil who was dark and very elegant.

Mme Lemesmil, who directed the fancy department, was herself like the very emblem of fancy and caprice, crowned by the curls and loops in which she dressed her hair. She was covered with jewels, necklaces, bracelets, brooches, and trinkets. She wore a multitude of elephants, number thirteens, little mills, sabots, tortoises, four-leaved clover, horseshoes, and playing cards. This arsenal of fetish silliness made around her a ceaseless and annoying clangour; it was just like her perfume, which was, I think, the most provocative carnation.

I had to manœuvre in the midst of these goddesses, and I had to summon up all my diplomacy to please everyone. M. Doucet had said to me: 'I am putting you in it as one throws a dog into the water to teach him to swim, you must manage as best you can.' . . . And I managed.

My first model was a little cloak in red cloth, with bands of cloth pinked round the neck. There was a lapel of the grey crêpe de Chine with which it was lined, and it buttoned up on one side with six enamel buttons. Four hundred copies were sold. Fair clients wanted it in every colour. Henceforth my position was assured.

One day I saw, arriving in her mule-drawn carriage, she who for me was the incarnation of all the genius, grace and spirit of Paris: Réjane. She was engulfed in the doorway with a great swishing of silk, and she asked for M. Doucet, who came to her, handsome as a god. She whispered into his ear about a new piece in which she was this and that, and M. Doucet, calling me up, immediately let me into their confidence: they were going to do *Zaza*. It was the story of a famous café-concert star who, after beginning her career amidst difficulties, found, at the height of her fame, a former lover at the door of her music-hall; she was to wear a grand and voluptuous mantle capable of impressing and electrifying not only this young man but the whole audience, and I was commissioned to make it. From that moment I could not sleep, none of my ideas seemed to me beautiful enough or in any way worthy of Réjane. Finally, I did make a cloak. It was of black tulle, veiling a black taffeta that had been painted by Billotey (a fan-painter then famous) with immense white and mauve irises; an enormous ribbon of mauve satin and another of violet satin running across the tulle joined the shoulders and closed the cloak in front with a cunning knot. All the sadness of a romantic dénouement, all the bitterness of a fourth act, were in this so-expressive cloak, and when they saw it appear, the audience foresaw the end of the play . . . Thenceforth, I was established, chez Doucet and in all Paris. I had stormed the ramparts on the shoulders of Réjane.

Chez Doucet I saw file by all the stars, all the glories of the epoch: Marthe Brandès, Theo, Mary Garden, Reichenberg, and my taste for the theatre was intensely delighted when we had the luck to dress a revue like that given each year at the *Epatant*, in the Rue Boissy d'Anglas. One year, we had to dress the *corps de ballet* of the Opera as soldiers of the First Empire. I went to Edouard Detaille to ask for information about the uniforms of the hussars of 1815, those soldiers who wore a jacket bordered with astrakhan, laced and braided, and on their heads kolbachs, with forage bags and sabretaches: M. Doucet had given me an introduction to Edouard Detaille. I found him painting a battle picture in his courtyard, where there was a cannon surrounded by members of the Central Brigade who were serving as models, disguised as artillerymen of the Empire. I told him the object of my visit, and almost without turning round he reeled off to me by heart the details of the colours of all the regiments of hussars in 1815, without forgetting the pipings and the lace. Then he showed me his imposing collection of costumes, sabres, and helmets. I returned home pondering the interest of this sort of extreme specialisation, and the beauty of a career given to the service of a single idea.

The rehearsals at the *Cercle de l'Epatant* filled me with joy. I saw the members of the *Cercle* press around the dancers, knock at the doors of the dressing rooms, and privily put flowers and notes into the hands of the valets. Hidden in a corner in the wings during the show, I saw M. Martel play a barrow-man of Aix-les-Bains, and I heard Mily Meyer sing the couplets written by the Marquis de Massa:

> *'There was once on a time a riding lady,*
> *There was once a Prince of Bavaria:*
> *The fair one was not made of stone*
> *And the Prince he was not of wood.'*

It referred, I think, to the loves of a sovereign and Cléo de Mérode.

I cannot describe the Maison Doucet without mentioning M. de la Pena, who for long was one of its chiefest lights. He was a very elegant man, slender, tall, incisive and dry, like Don Quixote himself, but a Don Quixote of rich and subtle aspect, with the grace of a fencer, and very demonstrative gestures, wasp-waisted (it was the day of corsets), his waistcoat puffed out over his chest, and immense handkerchiefs of very fine silk, coloured like parrots' tails, flowering from his pockets. M. de la Pena wore a short beard of impeccable cut and blackness, and the parting in the centre of his hair was carried right down to the neck. His clear, meticulous silhouette compelled me to admire him. He was Spanish, he could not be understood clearly, he spoke volubly, in a nasal voice.

I have seen him turning about some woman with his hands full of ribbons, laces, satins, velvets; it was like some incantation, some dance of flame: a ritual ceremony that lasted ten minutes, or sometimes even two hours, but from which the woman would depart arrayed, enriched, consecrated like an idol, for he displayed a talent, an ingenuity, and a skill that were marvellous – he has it all still, although the constraint of the financiers keeps him afar from the theatre of fashion. If you have not seen M. de la Pena pinning on ribbons with enchanted hands, modelling and draping and cutting out, with the great scissors he produced from his pocket, in a fire of inspiration, satins, taffetas, tulles and muslins, you cannot understand the joy and intense excitement that fill a true creator of fashion.

I was greatly struck by the mastery as much as by the chic of M. de la Pena, but what above all captivated me was the subtle simplicity and the natural richness of the elegance of M. Doucet. When I studied him I asked myself whence came that noble bearing and lofty grace. When he wore a dark blue suit one would have thought it had been dyed for him with a special blue, and his ties were of colour and texture as if the stuff had been woven by fairies. I promised myself that I would find out the address of his tailor, and one day I found it on the collar of one of his overcoats. It was Hammond, in the Place Vendôme. I passed many times in front of the shop of this English master without daring to cross the threshold. One day, when I was feeling in cavalier mood, and since I needed a suit, I went in and ordered one, not, however, without asking the price, through fear of some unpleasant surprise. I was told one hundred and eighty francs – and I gave my order.

'When shall I come to try it on?' I added (for I was eager to astonish my friends).

'Our clothes are made in London,' I was told, 'and yours will not be ready for seventeen days.'

I made an appointment and withdrew, thinking that one was wrong not to go oftener to the great houses, which after all, were not noticeably dearer than the others, and in seventeen days I returned.

Filled with emotion in the fitting room, I saw my coat arrive in the hands of the classic tailor, wearing a measure round his neck. I was astonished that they did not try on the trousers. He called the man who had received me, and the latter said to me: 'The trousers, Monsieur? What trousers? You did not order any trousers, nor a waist-coat either.'

A victim of the surprise I had feared, I was none the less forced to order both, in order to have a presentable *ensemble*.

At Doucet's we created new models each week. The belles of that day exhibited them at the races on Sundays, and they refused to admit the possibility that they could ever appear in a toilette that had already been seen. One remembers their names: Liane de Pougy, Emilienne d'Alençon, La Belle Otéro were then fêted by all the fashionable Grand Dukes and sovereigns; and then Nelly Neustratten, Marthe Helly, Germaine Thouvenin, Marguerite Bresil, and then Gaby de Naval and Liane de Lancy, etc. . . . Naturally, they waited until the last minute to order and try on the dress which was to make a sensation on the Sunday, and not infrequently it had to be impro-vised as late as Saturday evening, or, as I have seen done, it had to be hurriedly built up on the lady herself on Sunday morning. I liked to stay in Doucet's salons on Saturday evening, at the hour when the deliveries for Sunday were being prepared. Thus I had beneath my eyes, and even between my hands, all the dresses that would amuse Paris twenty-four hours later: I examined them as a connoisseur, I tested their stuff between my fingers, and it gave me extreme pleas-ure. On the following day I would go myself and study the bearing and port of these priestesses of elegance. I would ponder new models, more astonishing, more striking.

One day M. Doucet sent for me to his office. For me this was each time an occasion for fresh emotion, and great pride. Generally, he asked me about my new models, and went into them with criticism and corrections that always astonished me by their sureness and clarity. If I showed him a little tailor-made costume, he would find it too dry, seize from a nearby table a little bit of pea foulard, and twist up a cravat and apply it with a gesture full of distinction to that precise point where it would give a gay and decorative note. It gave my work a feeling of life and delicacy without which it would have been nothing.

In him I really felt I had my master, and I still think it was a great honour to have been his pupil. On that day he did not ask me about my models; he summoned me to say that he was pleased with me, to encourage me, and to give me my first salary. It was five hundred francs a month. It was an enormous sum at that time for a young man of my age, and when I related this event to my father the same evening – searching his eyes for the effect I should produce – he simply refused to believe me:

'Five hundred francs for a young man who knew nothing and had everything to learn . . . And,' he added, 'I am quite happy about it, you will not get the money!'

I replied to him: 'You're wrong, I have already pocketed it.'

'Very well, let me see it.'

And that was where the fun began, for instead of bringing out of my pocket five blue banknotes, I showed him sleeve links I had bought as I left the Maison Doucet, at a jeweller's in the Rue de la Paix. I had chosen them of the same kind as I had seen M. de la Pena wear; they were cabochon opals. I still wear them, in memory of the upbraiding I got from my father on that day: 'I had no notion of economy . . . I should finish in utter want . . . I was not providing for the future . . . etc.' Perhaps he was right . . .

I threw myself into the work more ardently than ever, stimulated by M. Doucet's appreciation. I composed a whole collection of costumes, which consisted of jackets and skirts drawn in at the waist. The women wore them over corsets that were real corselets, sheaths in which they were imprisoned from the throat to the knees; thence the skirts fell to the ground in a number of pans. I still have the drawings I made at that time, and to-day I would not dare to show them. None the less, they pleased. The agents for the buying houses tore them from one another.

These agents were not, as they later became, pirates and copyists who agree among themselves to buy only one dress among ten persons, and then to lend out the model among one another, imposing their taste on the Parisian houses, and forcing on them lines of the American mode that is always sterile and muttonish. I am speaking of the time when they came in great numbers to watch all the parades in the great houses. Twice a week the boats regularly unloaded them at Havre, and without losing a minute they hurried to the Rue de la

Paix, chez Worth, chez Paquin, chez Doucet; they looked on with wisdom, honesty, piety, at the paraded collections, then they always gave orders, and did not try to get out of it by promising to come back later. Yet many of them made fortunes in that period. I remember the great figures, Mme Hagué, Mme Benson. I am still grateful to them for having shown interest in my audacities. There were also private clients, like Mme Baldwin, and Mrs Langtry, and fair Parisiennes like Mme de la Villeroux, Mme Gaston Verdé de l'Isle, and many others.

And there were also some comic pieces, like that Baroness H—— who looked like an aged stable- or washer-woman, and who dragged in her wake the Baron and her little Loulou Pomeranian dogs. Looking like a drawing by Caran d'Ache, she marched in with an authoritative air and stared insolently at everyone. When she tried on her dresses in the little box reserved for that purpose she plied her cutter with privy smiles. She was continually seeking ways of attacking and humiliating the Baron, who had to hold the little dogs in his arms. If he let one slip she traced in the air a box on the ears. She would watch him and observe him in the mirror with a crushed expression, and turning toward him, full of sweetness and solicitude, she would say:

'Blow your nose, Henri.' And the Baron, putting down the dogs, would blow his nose.

One day she asked the cutter and myself to do the trying on at her house. The cutter was a Hungarian called Dukès, who had his hour of fame, but whose French I could never understand. She received us in her room, with the passive chaperoning of the Baron, to whom she suddenly said: 'Go and get some cigars for these gentlemen.' And the poor man went off lamely, dragging his gouty feet, and came back a few moments later with two cigars. As he was offering them to us, she knocked them into the air with the back of her hand, saying to him: 'Not those, you fool, though they are good enough for you.' And she herself went to fetch two boxes of cigars which, she said, were better, and she gave one to the cutter and one to me, with a smile that had no goodness in it. When we departed, I swore in my heart that no woman would ever treat me in such fashion, and that I would be on guard all my life to make myself respected by the fair sex.

People began to talk of me, and to recognise my creations and speak of them by my name. I became aware of my own personality. One day as he was chatting familiarly with me, M. Doucet said: 'My dear fellow, I don't see you going out enough. I have given you a very good salary, and it is in order that you may establish for yourself some small notoriety in Paris. If I see that you have not got enough money, I will help you. I should like to see you going to first nights at the theatre, going to the races, going to all the chic places with some little friend, some graceful girl whom you should dress according to your own taste, and for whom you should select a style. Perhaps they advise you at home to buy gilt edged securities, that is not what one must do if one wants to become a *couturier*. You can save later.'

This advice plunged me into great expectancy: I waited only for an opportunity to follow it, and in Paris such opportunities do not ever lack. I had the courage one day to tell my father of M. Doucet's proposals, and, although he would have liked to have appeared sickened and scandalised, he really understood very well, underneath, that the profession of a *couturier* is not incompatible with a certain experience of women – and I saw that he accepted the sacrifice of his opinions.

A few days later a surprise awaited me. I was given a letter from a client of the Maison Doucet, in which she asked me to join her at the Café de Paris, in a room on the first floor, where she had an urgent communication to make to me. She was an American actress who sang Viennese operettas in New York. I found her in that sumptuous setting, so well known to all the great gourmets of the whole world. It seemed to me as I crossed the great room on the ground floor that all the habitués were looking at me and studying me. I went up the stairs four at a time to get away, and I found Mrs —— at the door of a room, beautiful and smiling in a cloud of muslin. Beside her, her negress lady's maid, with a great Madras on her head, grinned happily with all her teeth. My lovely client, whom I had seen the previous day in my salons without any inkling of the favours she intended for me, drew me to her familiarly, and kissed me passionately on the mouth, before inviting me to lunch. The negress discreetly disappeared, and I knew all the intoxication of Joseph in the arms of Madame Potiphar. My new friend made me promise to follow her to Trouville, which was then the fashionable watering place, and the centre of Parisian life in the summer (for Deauville was created much later). I confided to her that I could not afford the expense: she advised me to address myself to M. Doucet, pointing out to him the interest he had in letting me follow the world of elegance at the great sporting events. Then she disappeared, forgetting and leaving behind on the restaurant table her little powder box that was of gold encrusted with diamonds. I asked for the bill: I was told it was already paid. I picked up the powder box, to give it back to her at Trouville, whither I betook myself next day.

Unconscious of the slightly risqué rôle I was being given to play, and drunk with pride, I went to the Hôtel de Paris, the finest and most expensive, and when I told them my name they replied: 'Quite so, Monsieur, there were no rooms left, and we have rigged up an apartment for you with screens in a passage. You will not have a view of the sea, but you will be very comfortable.'

I went up to my floor, and I found that, as if by chance, I was located precisely in front of the door of Mrs ——. As soon as I had dressed I went down to dine at a little table, and a few yards from me I saw my lovely friend, surrounded with elegance and riches, having on her right the Duke of —— and on her left Prince ——. It was not yet the moment to give her back her powder box, inside which I had found three thousand-franc notes, tightly folded. I dare not go at greater length into the details of this adventure, which gave a fragrance to my youth, and taught me English.

For five or six months I lived a disordered life, turn and turn about playing Romeo and cherub. As I was living at Billancourt at that time, I went on my bicycle every evening to the Avenue d'Iéna, where my lovely one lived in a magnificent apartment. The concierge eyed me when he saw me standing my dusty bicycle – we called them veloci-pedes then – at the foot of the stairs. I would arrive at her door; the negress, smiling and clucking, would seize hold of me to undress me, and made me put on a night-shirt that did not belong to me, and that bore over the heart an initial magnificently embroidered, and sur-mounted by a princely coronet. I had never seen a night-shirt like it. It was of dark blue silk with great white peas; the shirt-makers of to-day are children, who have let the secret of such marvels be lost.

My beloved would arrive. Should I avow that she was sometimes accompanied by a certain exalted personage; there were a few whis-perings with the negress, and she would pour out for the Gentleman a blackish beverage which might very well have been a Cordial

Médoc. Then she went to the piano, sang a couple of songs to rejoice her Prince, and gently urged him towards the door, without any resistance from him. Then, but then only, she threw herself into my arms . . . I do not know how I have come to tell you this story, that does so little to enhance my reputation. I ask the reader's indulgence only because of my youth.

These escapades had sown in me a taste for independence, and had strengthened my sense of the rights of my personality. I had frequent scenes with my father; decidedly we did not get on together, all the more because the Dreyfus *affaire* had come between us. My father had a horror of the Jews; I . . . I did not yet know any and, naturally, I was a Dreyfusard. It was the occasion for some pretty unpleasant collisions, which obliged me several times to leave my parents' house. Then I would take with me my books and all that belonged to me, and I would hang in my friends' houses the first pictures I had bought, especially those of the old painter Desbrosses, a pupil of Chintreuil, of whom I had four canvases – for which I paid by hard-saved monthly instalments: I was already a collector, like M. Doucet himself.

Soon, too, I was to leave the Maison Doucet; pretexts were certainly not lacking. I had designed for my *belle amie* new toilettes and models which I drew in the course of our conversations, at table or driving. She complained of the expensiveness of the great houses. She had taken my designs to a little dressmaker, where she had her dresses made. This came to the ears of M. Doucet, and that was one of his arguments for depriving himself of my services.

There was another: it was the time when *l'Aiglon* was being given, and I had designed most of the costumes, notably that of Sarah Bernhardt, all in white, with the scarf knotted at the waist that characterised the rôle. Because of this I frequently saw Mme Bernhardt, and one evening I thought myself authorised to cross the threshold of the playhouse where *l'Aiglon* was being rehearsed. Aided by the dusk I slipped into the stalls with a friend who was accompanying me. Round me I could make out a few people sunk in their seats. I could not recognise them. I heard a whole act of this piece, which was then unknown to all, and when the moment of Wagram came, when the troops filed by, reduced to a few representatives, I turned towards my friend and said to him in a low voice some remark as to the grotesqueness of the revue. My observation was overheard, and I know that it was remembered. My presence became known, the rehearsal was stopped, and Mme Sarah Bernhardt was told. M. Rostand informed her there were strangers in the house. Mme Sarah Bernhardt complained to M. Doucet of my indiscretion, which also became one of the causes of my disgrace.

One thing only disturbed me; the idea that I had angered a man whose opinion I revered, and that I had deserved to fall from his esteem. Happily I knew that he did not bear a grudge against me, and later I had evidence of the attachment he still felt for me.

III
In the Army

Two months later I had to fulfil my military obligations, and for a long year give myself to the service of my country. At that time there was three years' service, but there was a whole category that received dispensation. Some were the sole support of families, others belonged to certain institutions. I was myself a former pupil of the Institute of Living Oriental Languages, where Modern Greek, Tamil, Hindustani, Malagash, Javanese, and Arabic were taught; and in virtue of this my period of military service was limited to ten months. This seemed to me very long. One cannot jump at one bound from a life devoted to luxury and elegance to that low and wearisome existence which is the soldier's.

When I arrived at my regiment, I was lodged in the barracks of the Champ-de-Mars, at Rouen. I chose a bed right against the door, in order to have the feeling that I was almost free. At that time we soldiers had beds made of three planks on an iron base. On it I slept well, but from the first morning, when the bugle awoke me at half-past five, in the darkness, my first thought was for my mother, my house, my precious stuffs, and all that I idealised, and from which I had had to tear myself away.

I perceived at once the vanity of military life, for as I was the first in the order of the beds, it was my turn to light the lamp and to sweep; the Corporal shouted: 'The room-man, light the lamp, sweep under the beds.' I pointed out to him politely that there wasn't a lamp, but he had been two years in barracks, and answered me: 'I don't care a ——; light the lamp!' It was a revelation of the ancestral traditions that have always flourished in this picturesque *milieu*.

A little while after all those who, like myself, had dispensation – that is were exempted from two years' service – were assembled in a special platoon at the Pelissier Barracks. I found myself in a more select circle. My comrades were called Trairieux, de Vogüé, de Lesseps, Gilou, Alcan, P. Istel, O. Jalu, etc. . . . One day when we had made a long march in the rain, and had just returned tired out and wet through, we were ordered to attend a parade brushed, polished, and clean. But how could one clean and polish boots soaking with water and mud? While the best soldiers exerted themselves to rub themselves up, I suggested that we should all go down exactly in the state we were in, and I added: 'The Lieutenant will see that it is obviously not a case of bad will on our part.' I had reckoned without the military mind. We went down, some polished up, others with their shoes plastered with mud.

When the company was assembled, the Lieutenant called me out of the ranks all alone. He said to me: 'Private Poiret, I have just been told of what you said in the barracks, and the more I think about it, the more revolting I find your action. You were heard to say: 'If we all agreed amongst ourselves not to polish, nothing would be said to us.' Is there any need to point out to you the incongruity and also the scandalous nature of these words? In other terms, they signify that if the soldiers could unite to resist an order, their commander would be powerless. You have tried to introduce the right of striking into the Army. That is very, very grave; and I cannot but give you an exemplary punishment – for I ask myself where this sort of thing might stop. For myself, I give you eight days in the guardroom, and I should not be surprised if the Commandant increased it, and I think that the Colonel, who does not like obstinate fellows, will not fail to salt you well.'

And he lost himself in general disquisitions as to the right to strike, and anarchy. He was called Chauveau-Lagarde; one of his ancestors had deserved the honour of giving his name to a street in Paris.

From that day I doubted whether I were a good citizen, and my conscience as a soldier was shaken. I had lost my faith, and any hope of winning stripes through my deserts, and I had acquired the certainty that I and the military would not understand one another. I became a poor soldier, and got out of everything I possibly could. In the Infirmary, of which I became an habitué, I displayed singular maladies; my temperature rose as soon as the doctor had left, and reached a disquieting height; and returned to normal again as soon as he reappeared. Disquieted by these symptoms, the doctor did not hesitate to diagnose malaria, and sent me to hospital. There I became acquainted with the regulation purge, and the ridiculous uniform, composed of enormous shoes, floating pyjamas of chestnut baize bordered with red, and a cotton bonnet. It was rather like the costume of convicts.

One Sunday morning I was attending Mass with the good Sister who was in charge of the ward, in a neighbouring chapel, and I made of her an ally who helped me to obtain what I sought – convalescent leave.

The head of the hospital visited us each morning at six o'clock, with his assistants. He showed them my spleen and my liver. He wanted to see in them proof of an intermittent fever contracted in unhealthy country: in order not to gainsay him I had to say that I had lived in the neighbourhood of Rome, which I knew was marshy. 'Ah! You see!' he said, in triumph, and added: 'If that continues, I shall perform a punction of the spleen.' And that was why next morning, when he came on his rounds, he found me up, and when he asked me how I was, I told him that I felt a great deal better. For which reason he gave me convalescent leave for several weeks, which, prolonged in Paris, gave me the opportunity to return to designing and to the study of what pleased me: feminine elegance.

When I returned to the regiment, there was talk of having a fête to celebrate the centenary of Valmy, I think, or something of the sort, and I suggested to my comrades that I should write a revue in three acts, in which all the elements of military life should appear. In our barracks courtyard a theatre was constructed out of any available material. I had wide authority over the troupe, to which everyone wanted to belong, in order to get off parades. Beneath the eyes of the Prefect of Rouen and of the General Commanding the District, we played the revue, of which the subject was: The French Army (personified by your servant) welcoming a part-exempted recruit, the young Count du Bouton de la Bretelle, and initiating him into the charms of military life: the stew, the orderly room, fatigues, etc. . . . All these entities came on, and sang their couplets.

During the interval, the General, who was very Parisian, and whose name was Gallimard, came behind the scenes, congratulated me, embraced me, and offered me a glass of champagne, which I drank on his knee, like a light singing woman. I had faked up some patriotic couplets which reconciled me to the Commandant, and I was no longer considered an anarchist.

I will not go so far as to say that all was now fairweather sailing, but still, I have a number of pleasant recollections. I want to speak of one, which is of Private de C—— who, because of his talent as a pianist, was the General's special drummer and who, when he was admitted to his intimacy, became piano teacher to one of his daughters and the fiancé of the other. From that moment he was seen no more in barracks. He led the life of a turtle dove and cooed at all hours, or else one would meet him in the town wearing the General's boots with their golden spurs, riding on the General's own horse, and followed by one of the General's orderlies. He would be coming back from a ride in the forest, bearing flowers for his lady. On the day mobilisation was ordered, pianist and fiancé disappeared for ever: de C—— went back to England, where he lived, and where he later became, as I learned, the husband of Mme Steinheil, who had been released from prison.

IV
Chez Worth

At the end of my military service, I thought of returning to my habitual occupations, and I wanted to get into dressmaking again. The best way of getting back into touch with the great houses was to become a designer once more. I returned to my former clients, and especially M. Worth.

The Maison Worth at that time was directed by the two sons of the great *couturier* who had dressed the Empress Eugénie. They were called Jean and Gaston. It was Gaston who made me the following proposition:

'Young man, you know the Maison Worth, which has always dressed the Courts of the whole world. It possesses the most exalted and richest clientèle, but to-day this clientèle does not dress exclusively in robes of State. Sometimes Princesses take the omnibus, and go on foot in the streets. My brother Jean has always refused to make a certain order of dresses, for which he feels no inclination: simple and practical dresses which, none the less, we are asked for. We are like some great restaurant, which would refuse to serve aught but truffles. It is, therefore, necessary for us to create a department for fried potatoes.'

I perceived immediately what interest I might have in becoming the potato frier for this great house, and I at once accepted the position that was offered me. Its terms were, in any case, most flattering, and I began to make models that were severely criticised by the *vendeuses* (who reminded me of the Furies at Doucet's), but which pleased the public.

I got to know a type of dress that I had never before met with. I wanted to know everything that had been done before me, and several times I examined all the models successively. I even looked through the albums which told of the exuberances of good Father Worth the *couturier* of the Tuileries. They were full of samples and water-colour sketches, which spoke eloquently of the taste of the Court of the Empress. I especially remember a crinoline dress whose whole lower part was of telegraph wire, forming girandoles around which stuffed swallows flew and came to rest.

Another dress of the same period was garnished with great embroidered snails. I did not try to approximate my style to that of the House, but I must say that it had very much evolved, and that the dresses which came from the hands of M. Jean were models of art and purity. He worked a great deal after the pictures of the old masters, and I have seen him derive magnificent ideas from the canvases of Nattier and Largillière. He was surrounded by very highly skilled women, and by one, in particular, who moulded corsages as in the Great Century, out of plain or figured satin, which stood up stiff like armour, giving at the waist in charming folds to disclose the suppleness of the thighs. And he would make a sleeve out of a long tulle scarf held above the elbow by a row of diamonds and finished by two emerald tassels. (For he could not conceive that a dress could be made without some opulence.) I can understand very well why my little man-in-the-street lucubrations seemed to him wretched and puny.

M. Jean Worth was not very pleased at having introduced into his House an element which, in his opinion, lowered it. He did not like me very much, because in his eyes I represented a new spirit, in which there was a force (he felt it) which was to destroy and sweep away his dreams. When I was showing him a model, a little tailor-made, I saw him suddenly pale, as if he were going to be ill (he was extraordinarily nervous) and he pronounced, standing before his customary audience of obsequious courtiers, the following words:

'You call that a dress? It is a louse.'

And I, lest he should enlarge upon his theme, went off to hide my shame in my office. But this louse made its own way, and sold many times over; there must have been stormy arguments about me between the two brothers. I felt that I was hated by the one, supported by the other. Gaston Worth, who thought only of commercial results, foresaw the present day, and the threat that already overhung the Courts of Europe.

One day the House was filled with red velvet, and no other word was heard but Crimson. It was the colour of the cloaks of State at the Court of England, and the forthcoming coronation of Edward VII had been announced. M. Jean Worth proudly showed me a notice received from the English Court, describing the etiquette. All the nobility wore, according to their titles and precedence, longer or shorter trains, and more or less numerous ermine borders. For three months we made nothing but Court mantles. They were distributed throughout every room in the House, for one could not think of working on tables these fragile velvets, woven according to secular tradition – they would have been ruined if they had been pulled about. They were therefore placed over wooden mannequins, and their trains pinned to the floor; swarms of workwomen circled about them, working at pressure but meticulously, like arch-deacons around some holy relic. M. Worth showed everyone these hieratic masterpieces, which to him seemed to represent the superlative of beauty. He exulted. I must avow, with shame, that I never understood what he found admirable about them. I compared these conventional get-ups with the red, gold-fringed draperies held high by the Maison Belloir over important marriages, or distributions of prizes, in municipal ceremonies.

One day M. Worth was looking out of the window in the Rue de la Paix; he loved to see the coming and going of the carriages that brought to him the flower of the whole world. It was his familiar custom. Suddenly he turned round as if a spring had been released, saying:

'Mesdames, Princess Bariatinsky!'

And I saw that his heart was beating more quickly.

All the *vendeuses* rose with one movement, the chairs were ranged along the wall, as if for a revue, and everybody went toward the landing stage outside the lift. From every corridor there came forth members of the staff, who had been hastily informed. The whole House was on deck, in Indian file, in front of the door, and M. Worth stifled with his hands the barks of the little dog he was holding under his arm and which, stirred by the commotion, wanted to take part in the general rejoicing. I was at the end of the Indian file, curious to see the beautiful Princess who was the cause of this sensation. The lift took an immense time to come up, doubtless it was bearing a heavy weight. When it arrived at the landing, I was disillusioned to see in its interior nothing but a sort of fat little curate, black clad, with congested face, bent double over two sticks, and smoking a big cigar. Everyone bowed or curtseyed. M. Worth prostrated himself. The

Princess, in a voice full of assurance, said to him with the most perfect Russian accent:

'Worth, show me your confections.'

It was thus that she referred to the gowns.

M. Worth most obsequiously made her sit down, while the mannequins appeared with speed, and I had the honour of showing the Princess a cloak I had just finished, and which was then a novelty. Today it would seem banal, almost outmoded, but then nothing like it had been seen. It was a great square kimono in black cloth, bordered with black satin cut obliquely; the sleeves were wide right to the bottom, and were finished with embroidered cuffs like the sleeves of Chinese mantles. Did the Princess have some vision of China, which for Russia bore a hostile face? Did she see Port Arthur, or something other? I know not, but she cried out:

'Ah! What a horror; with us, when there are low fellows who run after our sledges and annoy us, we have their heads cut off, and we put them in sacks just like that . . .'

I already felt that my head was in the sack. I disappeared, cast down and despairing of ever pleasing Russian Princesses.

Soon after that an opportunity presented itself whereby I could make, in Paris, the dresses I best liked for the women I most esteemed. Premises in the Rue Auber were falling vacant. And a *vendeuse* from a neighbouring House was also about to be disengaged. I began to feel my wings spread, I had followed the advice of M. Doucet, and I had taken a pretty mistress, who was much remarked for the elegance with which I decked her out; I would try my luck.

At that time I was living at Auvers-sur-Oise, where I had hired a little house, typically the little suburban castle, in which I lived an independent and whim-directed existence. My little garden went down to the Oise, where I could fish in the morning before going to my work. I already had all the faults which have followed me throughout life, and have always been more precious to me than my good qualities. I was a free spender, I loved good cheer. My little friend, an Alsatian girl, had a great liking for cooking. I remember she would get up at five in the morning in order to souse the *hors d'œuvres* which were to be ready for lunch. She prepared the anchovies and fillets of herring, and when she came back to bed, she brought with her the fresh fragrances of thyme, of the morning, of chervil, and of chives.

These humble housewife cares did not prevent her from dressing with great elegance and piquancy. I remember a costume of black cloth with a little black pelerine that stopped at the shoulders, like Werther's tunic. She wore it with a little black tri-horned hat surmounted by a white cock's head with red comb. It was a delight, and I think it would still be found pretty to-day. All the women admired it, and made me understand that they would have gladly bought, if I would have sold.

One day I arrived from Auvers in M. Gaston Worth's office, and I said to him:

'You asked me to create a department for fried potatoes. I have done it. I am satisfied with it, and I hope you are too. But it spreads through the House an odour of frying, which appears to incommode a great many people. I therefore think of setting up for myself in another quarter, and frying chips on my own account. Will you pay for my frying pan?'

M. Worth smiled, and said he understood my impatience, and he congratulated me on my initiative, but he could not dream of taking an interest in any other business but his own, and in the pleasantest way in the world he wished me good luck.

V
My Debut as a *Couturier*

At No. 5, Rue Auber, at the corner of the Rue Scribe, there were premises which to-day are half the Kirby-Beard shop; they belonged to a tailor who had not succeeded. That did not frighten me. I resolved to set up my business there. My father, who might have put obstacles in the way of my impulse, was no longer there to steady me. My mother, who saw in my eyes the fire of the enthusiasm that engenders success, advanced me 50,000 francs. It was with this small capital that I made all the money I have since earned, and also that far larger amount I have since lost . . .

In a week the melancholy half-shop I had taken over had become spruce and gay. Oh, no, I had not committed any extravagances. My fittings were summary. I had had to keep, for economy's sake, the frightful carpet that I shall never be able to forget, rioting with fat red roses like red beefsteaks. But the public had eyes for my dresses only, I alone suffered. Lively window displays refreshed the sight of passers-by. Parisians of that day will recollect having stopped in front of my windows, to admire the cascading nuances I laid out in profusion. When autumn came I brought back from the Forest of Fontainebleau a carriage full of foliage, golden, burnt by the sun, and I intermingled it in my window with cloths and velvets carefully assorted. When it snowed, I called up all the faëry of winter by white cloths and tulles and muslins intermingled with dead branches, and I dressed the passing moment with an appositeness that ravished all who walked by in the street.

In a month I was known, and all Paris had stopped at least once before the shop that was henceforth famous. One day Réjane came, in her mule-drawn carriage. It was an event. She came back often. I had few employees, and amongst them a bookkeeper who swindled me, and who almost made my dreams come to shipwreck. The memory of Princess Bariatinsky haunted me, and the cloak she had reproved seemed to me more and more beautiful. It was to become the type of a whole series of creations. And might one not still say, to-day, that there is something of this model in the cloaks that are made everywhere? In any case, for years, it dominated and inspired the mode. I called it 'Confucius.' Every woman bought at least one. It was the beginning of the Oriental influence in fashion, of which I had made myself the apostle.

It was still the age of the corset. I waged war upon it. The last representative of this abominated apparatus was called the *Gache Sarraute*. It divided its wearer into two distinct masses: on one side there was the bust and bosom, on the other, the whole behindward aspect, so that the lady looked as if she were hauling a trailer. It was almost a return to the bustle. Like all great revolutions, that one had been made in the name of Liberty – to give free play to the abdomen: it was equally in the name of Liberty that I proclaimed the fall of the corset and the adoption of the brassière which, since then, has won the day.

Yes, I freed the bust but I shackled the legs. You will remember the tears, the cries, the gnashings of teeth caused by this ukase of fashion. Women complained of being no longer able to walk, nor get into a carriage. All their jeremiads pleaded in favour of my innovation. Are their protestations still heard? Did they not utter the same groans when they returned to fullness? Have their complaints or grumblings ever arrested the movement of fashion, or have they not rather, on the contrary, helped it by advertising it?

Everyone wore the tight skirt.

But these first successes were not very profitable to me because of the unfaithfulness of my bookkeeper, who deceived me as to the profits of the business. I experienced all the mortification of the novice. One day it was seen that several pieces of silk were missing, and as I had begun an investigation that had not produced any result, I thought of seeking information from occultism. This bizarre idea had been suggested to me by a former police commissary who told me that, in extreme and desperate cases, he had obtained precious revelations from clairvoyants. After trying to dissuade me from having recourse to this procedure, my bookkeeper asked permission to accompany me to the clairvoyante I had chosen, who was of the cheaper sort. She lived in the depths of a court, and received us in a little kitchen where there was a cat and water singing over the fire, as if she were indeed a witch. When she had gone into a trance she told me that I had been the victim of a theft, and that she was going to tell me of the circumstances in which it had been committed:

'I see two men,' she said, 'with a push cart, who stop in front of your shop. It is Sunday morning, the street is almost empty. One of the two has the key of the shop front, he opens the little low door, and bends down to enter. He takes the pieces of silk and passes them to his accomplice. They go off together along a great Avenue, straight toward the west.'

My bookkeeper had the key of the door and lived at Houilles. He was profoundly disturbed by these revelations, which doubtless corresponded to what he knew. I asked the clairvoyante to show me more definitely the thief's face. Then she said to me: 'I don't know what is the matter with me. I seem to have difficulty in expressing myself. I feel embarrassed and ill at ease. The man has a high colour. He has red hair and is in your immediate entourage; he holds himself very upright. You would never believe that he is guilty.' I paid her the modest fee, and we went out. On reaching the bottom of the stairway I stood in front of my bookkeeper and prevented him reaching the door. I took him by his two arms, and staring him straight in the eyes, I said to him gently:

'What do you think about it?'

He replied that this method of investigation made him laugh, and he would prefer to give me notice, for he perceived clearly that I lacked confidence in him.

I had an office on the first floor which gave on to the Rue Auber, and my eyes had several times been drawn to the balcony of a neighbouring modiste, whereon I could see several attractive women. One above all seemed to me the most beautiful I had ever encountered. I can't remember under what pretext I attracted her to my house, but I know she caused me an immense disturbance when she came; she was brown-haired with blue eyes. What blue eyes! Myosotis! There was an irresistible attraction between us, and I know well that it was she who revealed to me all I know of love. She had a sort of husband, but neither she nor I were stopped a moment by that consideration, and we had sacrificed him by mutual consent without ever having spoken about it. Yet he would appear in front of us in the street, and piteously exhibit his misery to us, like a ghost. We were cruel and gay.

We would have overturned other obstacles, because we bore within us an irresistible force; I wanted to base my future on this foundation, which seemed to me to have been imposed on us by destiny, and I still ask myself why my designs came to naught. I can no longer remember. If these lines should fall one day beneath the eyes of Marthe, may she know of the piety, of the beauty, of the respect with which I keep the memory of the hours I lived with her. And may the reader pardon me this romantic digression.

It was at this time that I made the acquaintance of Bernard Naudin. I had seen drawings by him in the *Cri de Paris*, and, very simply, I had asked him to design for me some letter-headings. Then there was revealed to me what is the life of a real artist, consecrated solely to his work. I could not find any more lofty example of the love of art. I looked on at every part of his work, I knew all his dreams and all his hopes, I saw him attacking the great illustrations that made him famous; and I saw from close at hand the devouring passion that possessed him. In the modest apartment where he lived in the Rue du Laos or the Rue Nicolas-Charlet, I loved to find him at his work-table amongst his engraving tools, his copper and his acids, mastering his materials, pursuing the expression of his ideas. And then, when he had attained his end, he himself for himself procured his reward, by seizing a guitar suspended behind him and within reach of his hand, whereon he would execute indifferently a malagueña, or some air of Bach's; and one could pass the whole afternoon listening to him, if he let himself go, chanting with knowing smiles the ribald and clandestine songs of the seventeenth century. There was one especially, by the Abbé de Chaulieu, of which the little I remember still delights me. I am proud to have been and to be a friend of Naudin, who is one of the finest artists I have known, and I am proud to have given him that old viola da gamba from which he knew how to draw notes so pure that celebrated musicians like the Casadesuses did not hesitate to have him in their concerts. I shall have occasion to speak of him again further on. Au revoir, Naudin.

My reputation began to grow, but I was not entirely satisfied with my life, which spent itself in frivolous and unstable social relations. I had plenty of friends and pals, Desclers, Picabia le Fauve, who then was sagely copying Sisley, for instance, with whom I found amusement;

but it was only amusement, pleasure, and I dreamed of happiness. It was the period when opium dens were in full blast everywhere; the drug was beginning to be the fashion; invitations had been given me to go to certain naval officers, to certain artists, who lived in elaborate elegance, and initiated their friends into the delights of the narcotic. I always resisted their persuasions, and I am not sorry to have an opportunity of saying so here, in order to answer once and for all the insinuations and libels of allegedly well-informed persons, who have chosen to regard me as a pervert and a Satanist. My means did not allow me to be either one or the other; and I have never known either opium, or cocaine, or morphine; nor any poison of the body or of the soul. On the contrary, I pondered how to consolidate and secure my life which, in the special *milieu* in which I lived, was in some risk of becoming disordered and profitless. Family life appeared to me as a defence against this danger, and I sought to decide myself in favour of it.

I greatly astonished my people when I revealed my intention to them. I wanted to get to know again a friend of my childhood, who seemed to me the most suitable person to become my companion. It was pointed out to me that she was not a Parisienne, and that perhaps she would not have any dowry. She did, in fact, live in the country, far enough from Paris to have avoided contamination from the superficial education of those I went amongst, and that was what pleased me. She was extremely simple, and all those who have admired her since I made her my wife would certainly not have chosen her in the state in which I found her. But I had a designer's eye, and I saw her hidden graces. I observed her poses and gestures, and even her faults – which might be turned to advantage.

I remember her first visits to the Rue Auber, where she came with her mother. My employees (all Parisian women are not charitable) ill dissembled their astonishment at seeing me prefer to them this provincial who wore a black hat, flanked by a nosegay of white roses, and who, frankly, did not have the fashionable bearing. But I knew where I wanted to go.

A few months later, the miracle had begun. We were living in the Rue de Rome, where our nights were shattered by the whistles of the suburban trains. It was there that I began to receive artists, and to create around me a movement. We constantly went to antiquarians, and to museums, and we worked ceaselessly to enrich the cultivation of our minds, to sharpen our sensibilities. Then we travelled to study, and all the museums of Europe were familiar to us. Italy captivated us. At the contact of so much beauty my conquest became more precious, and transformed herself. She revealed herself to herself. She was to become one of the queens of Paris. Her appearance in elegant places was noted, and several times produced a real sensation. At the first performance of *Minaret*, by Jacques Richepin, she wore on her head a turban – a headdress that had not been seen on any Parisienne since Mme de Staël and, as if to accentuate the provocation to public opinion, this turban was surmounted by an aigrette, which must have been about a foot high. Mme Poiret was thenceforth established, and the little Parisian girls laughed at her no longer.

I soon left the Rue Auber, for it had become too small for my business and I installed myself in the Rue Pasquier, in a private house which, at very little expense, I had arranged to my taste. This pretension on the part of a dressmaker, who received his clients in a private house, without a shop-sign and without window display, was diversely interpreted. Slanderous tongues and the little blackmailing newspapers spread all the scandalous and stupid rumours one can imagine. They could not effect anything against my growing reputation, and I received *chez noi* all the great ladies of Paris and elsewhere.

It was there that Mrs Asquith came to see me, the famous Margot. She was already one of the most alive and vivid personalities in the life of London. I will not attempt to sketch her portrait. I will only recall that long nose, full of race, that sharp profile, that bitter and contemptuous mouth, close-lipped but always in movement, betraying all the changes in her thought, that lofty bearing, those rapid and capricious gestures: a sort of Sioux chief. And in the ceaseless movements of her face, a cold and observant eye, the incisive glance of a surgeon which, however, at moments, reflected an infinite gentleness and a great goodness.

She could neglect any effort to please because she imposed by her bearing, but she could only fascinate intelligent people, whose criteria are beyond the vulgar range.

She entered my salons like a thunder-clap, and while preparations were being made to show her my collection of dresses, she explained to me how she was accustomed to dress; and she showed me that she was wearing knickers, which were of violet satin. Then she watched the parade of my creations, and she seemed transported by the spectacle I offered her. She had never thought, she said, that such beautiful things could exist:

'Monsieur Poiret, Englishwomen must know your dresses. They are dresses for aristocrats and great ladies. I want to help you to reveal them to us. You will have an assured success. I am going to organise a tea, to which I shall invite my most elegant friends. Would you like to bring your mannequins and your dresses?'

That was crossing the Channel by a golden bridge; I accepted with enthusiasm and, a few weeks after, I set out with some mannequins and a collection of day and evening toilettes worthy of my hosts.

The day after our arrival we went to the fine house in Downing Street where Mr Asquith, the Prime Minister, lived, and while the trunks were being unpacked I looked through the windows at the machine-like Horse Guards doing sentry-go in the smoky courtyard of Whitehall.

The parade was a triumph. The audience was the finest I had ever seen. Mr Asquith came in for a moment; I was presented to him, then he went back to his study, his demeanour rather grave.

At seven in the evening there was a chill, and I was packed off without any standing on ceremony. In the street, some journalists lay in wait for me. Two taxis took on board the mannequins and the trunks, and we returned to our hotel without drums or trumpets. But next day, the trumpets rang out indeed.

Journalists had assailed me throughout the evening, asking me for confidential interviews, taking my photograph, and even questioning my mannequins as to the fashion in which Mrs Asquith had treated us. I had the key to these mysteries when the papers appeared with sensational headlines: 'An Exhibition at Gowning Street' (a play upon the name of the official residence of the Prime Minister), or else: 'French Trade Represented by the English Premier.' In one paper there was a huge photograph of Mr Asquith, and opposite, a huge photograph of myself. I learned that the exhibition the day before had been used in order to reproach Mr Asquith, who was a Free Trader, very severely for having lent his salons to a foreign merchant, and for having betrayed the cause of English trade. 'Not only does Mr Asquith refuse his own people the right of protection, but he facilitates the intrusion of foreign merchandise by organising exhibitions in the residence which has been paid for by the nation's trade!' The argument was a powerful one; it burst like a bomb; Mr Asquith was questioned in Parliament and was called to order by his party; Mrs Asquith, too, I think. As for me, I was launched in London.

I saw Mrs Asquith at a friend's in Paris, long after. The poor woman no longer dared to meet me. As a result of the indiscretion she had committed, she had been persecuted by the English tradesmen, and she had had to order dresses in all the shops in London to give them proof of her loyalty and fidelity. All her lovely friends came to me for their dresses. She alone dared not come. I assured her of the gratitude I felt toward her in every circumstance for the very sporting way in which she had borne the trials that were, to me, so profitable.

I met her more recently at Cannes, where I went every season, for it was little to have a fine house in Paris and be visited there by the high society of every country: I had to go whither went my clients, and hold myself ready to serve them in all their favoured holiday places. I had a branch at Deauville and one at La Baule; one at Cannes and one at Biarritz. The manner in which I had them fitted up was sometimes criticised. At Cannes in particular, I had found only a cellar: it was underneath the Cercle Nautique, and received air and light only through its front. I made it like a free and easy rural retreat, gay and seductive. All the passers-by craned their necks to cast a curious glance. A few days after the opening of this intriguing shop, which was lit by many coloured bells, a gentleman came in without taking his hat off, and, with a very decided air, walked to the other end of the room, whistling. Then, pushing aside a screen, he studied himself in a mirror, and, as dresses were being shown to some clients, he settled himself to observe the attitudes of the models. This was going too far. I went up to him and I said:

'Monsieur, I must ask you to observe that there are several ladies here, and that it is incorrect for you to keep on your hat . . .'

'I know what I have to do . . .' and he went out without touching his hat.

I was lunching that day at the Casino, and I was talking with Cornuché near the entrance to the dining-room when I saw the same personage arrive with important step. Some women who were sitting down at once rose and hastened to meet him, and kissed his hand, with a curtsey or a bow. Six times he received the homage of a newcomer, without showing any response and without replying by a single gesture to their eagerness and their devotion.

I questioned Cornuché, who told me:

'He is the Grand Duke Alexander . . .'

I had made another gaffe, but I did not regret it.

One morning Mrs Asquith, bending towards the windows of my shop in the Croisette, was admiring one of my little costumes. I came out to greet her. She invited me to lunch with Lady Booth, with whom she was staying. I accepted with my friend, the painter Oberlé, who was my guest. She forgot her invitation and did not come. This mannerism of hers astonished no one, and Lady Booth was more than charming in her welcome.

I met there several high personages in English society, notably Lord Lascelles, son-in-law of H.M. the King of England; and also a Member of Parliament, and a great lady whose name escapes me. The lunch was English, that is to say, bad and distinguished. As it was coming to an end, I was informed that Professor Akldar wished to speak to me. I asked that he should be requested to wait, for he was a magician whose real name was Kahn, and I did not think of introducing him into this chosen circle. I had to explain who he was. He was a clairvoyant who pierced with his gaze the secrets of envelopes and pockets, and who read letters folded up inside portfolios. I caused general curiosity, and they insisted that I should bring him in. He was waiting in the antechamber. At the general request I signed the order for his release.

Professor Akldar, as he came in, said to the Member of Parliament that he could see he was troubled by grave disquiet, relative to English policy in China, and he read him a letter which the M.P. had in his pocket, or at least indicated its tenor with so much exactitude that the Member, disquieted, asked him for an interview for which he paid, I found out afterwards, 10,000 francs.

After lunch I took my departure, and left the magician in conversation with someone or other in the party – I did not know who. A few weeks later I had the unpleasantness of receiving a letter from an old lady who complained that on that occasion I had presented to her this M. Kahn, whom she considered a rogue. She had, she said, made a bargain with him, and had given him a sum of 10,000 francs to bet at the races, for he had said he knew in advance the names of the winners. She was to have a 50 per cent interest in the winnings, but would not participate in the losses. He had bet as arranged, and won, as he had promised, a sum of 70,000 francs. But he had returned nothing to his partner, saying that the bargain was illegal. I was truly astonished that a great English lady could have accepted dealings of this order with a stranger, and above all, at the conditions she had introduced into her bargain, whereby she had an interest in the successful bets, but had nothing to do with the others. That definitely put her in a bad position, and prevented one from sympathising with her.

I communicated her letter to Mrs Asquith, protesting in my turn against this unjust accusation. She replied that the old lady was mad, and had been ever since she became the wife of a lord, an event for which nothing had prepared her. For she had spent her whole youth running about gathering simples in the fields for her father, who was a chemist (for Mrs Asquith had a charming irony).

VI
My Influence

People have been good enough to say that I have exercised a powerful influence over my age, and that I have inspired the whole of my
generation. I dare not make the pretension that this is true, and I
feel, indeed, extremely diffident about it, but yet, if I summon up my
memories, I am truly obliged to admit that, when I began to do what
I wanted to do in dress-designing, there were absolutely no tints left
on the palette of the colourists. The taste for the refinements of the
eighteenth century had led all the women into a sort of deliques-
cence, and on the pretext that it was 'distinguished,' all vitality had
been suppressed. Nuances of nymph's thigh, lilacs, swooning mauves,
tender blue hortensias, niles, maizes, straws, all that was soft, washed-
out, and insipid, was held in honour. I threw into this sheepcote a few
rough wolves; reds, greens, violets, royal blues, that made all the rest
sing aloud. I had to wake up the good people of Lyons, whose stomach is a bit heavy, and put a little gaiety, a little new freshness, into
their colour schemes. There were orange and lemon crêpe de Chines
which they would not have dared to imagine. On the other hand, the
morbid mauves were hunted out of existence: there appeared a
new dawn – the gamut of the pastel shades. I carried with me the
colourists when I took each tone at its most vivid, and I restored to
health all the exhausted nuances. I am truly forced to accord myself
the merit of all this, and to recognise also that since I have ceased to
stimulate the colours, they have fallen once more into neurasthenic
anæmia.

Women to-day imagine they can distinguish themselves and recognise themselves in the gamut of beiges and greys. On the contrary,
they are confounded in a nebulous fog, which will be the symbol of
our epoch. Fashion to-day needs a new master. It has need of a tyrant
to castigate it, and liberate it from its scruples. He who shall render it
this service will be loved, and will become rich. He will have to do
what I did then, and not look behind him, and consider nothing save
women and what becomes them. But once he has come to a conviction,

he must follow out his idea cost what it may, without paying attention to his rivals or bothering about being followed. He will not be followed the first year, but he will be copied the second.

But it is neither by restoring life to the colour scheme, nor by launching new styles, that I think I rendered the greatest service to my epoch; for what I did in that order of endeavour, perhaps another could have done. It was in my inspiration of artists, in my dressing of theatrical pieces, in my assimilation of and response to new needs, that I served the public of my day.

Let me recall to you the positive Revolution in the art of stage presentation and design that was effected by the first presentation of *Minaret*. I don't know how many performances the play had, but without any doubt, it owed a hundred of them to me. I seem to remember that its book was a poor thing, to which the author himself cannot have attached much importance; the real thing was the costumes and the scenes.

For the first time the dress designer and the scenic artists had co-operated, and had adopted the same conception. Contrary to all that had been done up to that time, when the dress designer had sent gowns to the theatre without knowing with what sauce they would be eaten, that is to say, beneath what lighting and on what background they would be served up, my friends Ronsin, Marc Henri, Laverdet and I were completely in agreement as to certain very simple dominant harmonies, whose limits we each undertook to respect. The first act was to be blue and green. The second, red and violet. The third, black and white. And I did not allow myself a single infraction of this pre-arranged scheme. When the curtain went up on the first act, the audience uttered a spontaneous 'Ah!' as if it had felt the freshness of the first raindrops of a long-needed shower. Everything melted into the same elementary gamut. There was no irrelevance of tones to weary the eye. We very carefully managed our effects in the second act, which was a troubling act, to which Mme Cora Laparcerie attached a great deal of importance. The contrast of its violence with the freshness of the beginning produced the fullest effect. Do you remember the red trees and the violet flowers, in which we had permitted ourselves golden highlights and black shadows? The dark, sumptuous richness of this ensemble made one think of the sound of some magnificent organ. It was impossible to increase the audience's emotion, save by the calm and tranquillity of the third act, which was why we treated it in black and white, and enriched it with pearls and diamonds. I still have a vivid memory of Galipaux in rich black and white, and it was with the formal assent and consent of Ronsin, my collaborator, that I allowed myself an apple-green costume for Claudius, in the rôle of the 'Eunuch,' which was a charming and acidulated licence. It was appreciated.

I don't know whether you will remember the setting I created a little while after for a small masterpiece by Rip called *Plus ça change* . . . which has been very many times adapted, dressed, and undressed, by divers artists. I have always worked in the same way, setting myself between the two extremes of two tones for each tableau. For instance, white and blue, or orange and lemon. In *Plus ça change* . . . there was an act that took place in the Middle Ages: in it Isabeau of Bavaria (Spinelly) appeared in a grandiose head-dress and her ladies-in-waiting in pointed bonnets. Charles VI, called The Fool, appeared and sang:

> *'I have done pipi into the sea*
> *To annoy the English fleet . . .'*

I chose blue and red to dress this scene, and to recall the illumination of incunabula and old missals. One could see upon the stage, at one and the same moment, every tone of blue and of red mingled with gold. Visualise the rich yet sober harmony it made. A casement, which formed the background of the scene, was treated in the same tones, and threw shadows of the same colour on to the floor.

I blush to have to relate my own triumphs and distinctions. I do it far less to recall the services I have rendered, than to seek out the causes that made me celebrated. I cannot forget in this connection the nights I passed at 'La Renaissance' at the rehearsals of *Aphrodite*, which all resolved themselves into an interminable discussion between Pierre Frondaie, the adaptor, and Cora Laparcerie. The real author, Pierre Louys, only came once, and he was not listened to. 'To H—— with you, Madame,' Pierre Frondaie would shout, raising his stick, and poor Cora would make a pretence of retiring into her box, where she further manipulated the defective play.

The adaptor, who had every kind of pretension and every kind of grossness, insisted that the lighthouse of Alexandria should be in the distance, and that it should be so made that men could be sent up into it. Thus there were to be seen on a little tower life-size persons, as in Giotto's pictures. The first night audience did not relish the joke. Ronsin and I were the only ones to find it amusing.

Several artists have given in their drawings a pretty accurate idea of the spirit of that time. I picked out especially Jean Villemot and Paul Iribe; the latter had founded a review, *Le Temoin*, which was edited with a great deal of wit and a distinctly new note. It was illustrated almost wholly by himself; I asked Iribe to meet me, and thus made his acquaintance.

He was an extremely odd chap, a Basque plump as a capon, and reminding one both of a seminarist and of a printer's reader. In the seventeenth century he would have been a Court abbé. He wore gold spectacles, and a wide open collar, around which was tied rather loosely a scarf of the sort affected by Mr Whitney Warren. He spoke in a very low voice, as if mysterious, and gave some of his words a special significance by separating their syllables; for instance, he would say, 'It is – ad-mir-able.' Altogether a charming and remarkable personality.

I confided to Iribe my plan of bringing out a very beautifully produced publication, intended for the élite of Society. An album of his drawings picturing my dresses, printed on the finest Arches or Holland paper, which should be dedicated in homage to all the great ladies of the whole world. Then, I made him look at my dresses, to observe his reactions; he all but swooned.

'I have often dreamed of dresses of this kind,' he said to me, 'but I had never supposed that anyone had already created them. It is ad-mir-able, and I want to set to work im-med-iately; I also want to bring to you an as-ton-ishing woman, of infinite distinction, who will wear these dresses div-ine-ly; it is Madame L——, the daughter of Bj—— Bj——; she is ravishing!' He brought her to see me a few days later.

Since by chance Iribe needed money, I paid him the amount due for his first drawings – and he disappeared. The time seemed long to me before he came back; I had forgotten to ask him his address. When he brought me his sketches, I was enchanted with the way in which he had understood and interpreted my models. And I asked him to finish his work rapidly, for it was important to offer to the sophisticated public we wished to reach a work of great freshness: it must therefore appear before the mode had changed. And first of all, I said to him, Give me your address, so that I may be able to correspond with you. He replied that he had no fixed address in Paris, but that he breakfasted every morning chez Madame L——. Then, having pocketed a new advance on account, he vanished once more.

This time I had a great deal of trouble in getting him back and obtaining delivery of his work. I think I remember that I had to threaten him rather seriously to make him finish the album. Finally, he sent me his last drawings, and the work of printing could begin. This work, which to-day is to be found in every artist's and art-lover's library, is well known. It is an ad-mir-able production, and it was then a document without precedent. It was carried out with so much wit that it is scarcely outmoded to-day. Its title was: '*Les Robes de Paul Poiret, racontées par Paul Iribe.*'

I am not unwilling to clear up here a point in my history that has been raised by a venomous Parisian paper, which has sought to insinuate that 'my personal genius' was naught else but the talent of Iribe and of Marie Laurencin. As far as the second is concerned, the suggestion is so absurd that it does not deserve examination; as far as it concerns Paul Iribe, I have written to him at an address I imagine will reach him (because he cannot any longer be breakfasting chez Madame L——) to ask him to send to the paper a correction – which has not yet appeared. I cannot believe that Paul Iribe seriously intends to contest with me the paternity of my work. That would be a clumsy piece of childishness, for I would not delay to confound him by setting before his eyes his sketch albums, which I have piously preserved. In them one can see the details of my dresses noted with scrupulous exactitude, and written indications that witness his care to respect my model.

But Paul Iribe is not, I think, among those who try to establish themselves in the nest of others, and there cannot be any question of polemic between us, if he does justice to my personality as I salute his. In any case, these lines are written without acrimony, and when I lift the veil from our youth, from his beginnings as from my own, I do not seek to cause him the slightest pain or embarrassment.

*

Two years after Iribe's album I asked Georges Lepape to make a simi-
lar one. He undertook it in the same fashion, he came to see my
creations, and drew them with verve. Lepape will not deny the part I
took in his work, and the influence I exercised over him: at that time
he was more or less unknown. I think I gave him a marvellous opportunity to reveal himself to the public in a kind that was precisely
suited to him, and I think I guided his taste. His fine career has jus-
tified me. It is perhaps in the ascendancy that I had over him and
others that my most efficacious influence is to be seen.

It was also at this period that I made the acquaintance of the
painter Boussingault. M. Jacques Rouché had asked me to write for
La Grande Revue an article of a few pages about 'La Grande Couture.'

It was an extraordinary honour for a dress-designer to be included
in an organ of this quality. I did not flee from it, and when my article
was written it was given to Boussingault, who was to illustrate it. Jean
Boussingault came to me one morning to ask me for information as
to the forms he should evoke. What a curious personage! Tall, elegant, carefully dressed, he had the rigid bearing of a cassowary. I
think that I could sketch his face by simply making a great nose sharpened like a beak, and two heavy eyelids beneath hair smoothed like
shiny feathers; and two avid and sensual lips, that yet were sober in
speech. He contributed, indeed, nothing to our conversation, he was
a shy contemplative. We became cronies and it was he who, on one of
his visits to me, introduced me to Dunoyer de Segonzac.

The latter is to-day famous enough not to need description: he
belongs to Parisian life, despite his great reserve and his anxiety not
to spread himself.

Segonzac was making his début pretty unsuccessfully; his great
canvases at the *Salon d'Automne* and the *Independents* had elicited
more attention than admiration. These chaoses of opened legs and
bits of arms presented pellmell in the grass intermingled with parasols, were taken to be illustrations of some obscure news item, and
sometimes aroused the indignation of the well-affected citizenry.
We often laughed together over the opinions we overheard in the
exhibitions, during our promenades around his canvases. Let us
admit it: he was misunderstood, and I must myself confess that,
when I bought his first pictures, I had more confidence in the man
than in the work. When I asked him to sell me his great canvas, *Les*

Buveurs, I astonished him very much. It had not been successful, and he had rolled it round a stick and put it away in some corner of his studio. That is what explains, because of the thickness of the paint, why it is covered with little waves and undulations. He scarcely dared to ask me a price, and when I proposed the figure of 3,000 francs, he burst out with his great hearty laugh, saying: 'If you like.' But ten years later this canvas was to reach the figure of 90,000 francs at the auction at the Hôtel Drouot.

Every kind of thing was said about this, notably that I bought it back myself to puff the name of my friend, or else that it was a fictitious sale. Truly the world is either stupid or malicious, or both! I consoled myself for my discomfiture when Segonzac's pictures officially attained the prices they deserved, and I congratulated myself on having been the occasion of this revelation to the public. I shall always be very proud of it, for Segonzac is to-day an august painter, who has a shorthand-secretary. His autograph is all the more valuable. I will not say that he is a pontiff. He would not pardon me, but I am forced to state that as he has become rich he has changed his habits and his friends. In those friendly reunions we frequently had, and in which he played a dominant rôle, as much because of the quality of his wit as because of the popularity he enjoyed, he scarcely appears to-day save like some meteor, or some busy Minister who stops a moment between two sittings of the Cabinet and of Parliament, shakes hands, and disappears in a cloud of sympathetic curiosity, or else glides out silently in the English fashion. I cannot but regret that delightful epoch when he was only Minister for Laughter, and when he would imitate simultaneously the Senator and the Farmer conversing at an agricultural show. What charming improvisations, full of life and colour! What racy impersonations of types he gave then! I have photographs of him taken at parties of mine, in which he always achieved for himself a striking success. I do not threaten him with their publication, for I do not wish to be disagreeable to him, but I hope that he will never disown this past, to which he owes his success of to-day. He had then all the psychological finesse, all the sharp irony of a Molière or a Beaumarchais. I often wonder whether he has let his dramatic verve rust, or whether he still gives it play before certain assemblies more worthy of it.

It has often happened to me to discover unknown talents, and to reveal to the public new names. In the theatre, I launched the little Dourga, the Hindoo dancer, and Vanah Yahmi, and Nyota Inyoka, who were turn and turn about Vishnu and Krishna. I made Caryathis and many others first known, but I never made so big a discovery as that of Dunoyer de Segonzac, unless it be that I made in London, last year, of Andrée Levy, still unknown to the public, but whose expressive, palpitating talent will soon force universal recognition, for nothing will be able to resist this force of nature. None of the 'stars' I have mentioned remained in contact with me; one by one they have been seen to pale, in proportion as they became more distant from my orbit; were they merely planets? Did they need my sun? I do not make that supposition, but yet I am certain that I provided them with the opportunity for unique work, and that I fertilised their talents by the openings and facilities I offered them. I took advantage of all their faculties, and I knew how to bring to light all their gifts; then, they became intoxicated with applause, and believed themselves already at the zenith of glory, and no longer took account of the importance of my collaboration. They thought they had arrived or, as one says in Paris, they thought *it* had arrived. They did not know, poor things, that glory renews and regilds itself each day, that an unceasing battle must be fought to retain the place one has acquired, and that every morning one must win a victory, if one desires to remain a 'star' of Paris.

Look at Mistinguett. Does she not fight the good fight every night to keep her place? I have a limitless admiration for the desperate effort she puts forth. It is like the labour of an insect, rebuilding again each day its nest destroyed by the public's kick. Nothing is more moving than this struggle, and nothing is less laughable. Here and now I defend this artiste, although once she played me a truly unpleasant trick: In a revue at the *Casino de Paris*, I had undertaken to make the costumes for a sketch entitled *The Weapons of Woman*, and in it Mistinguett represented *The Rose*. I made her a ravishing costume that cost more than ten times the price I was to receive, but I had let myself be carried away by my desire to realise a beautiful thing. The rose really was A Rose.

It was a crinoline skirt made of immense petals that flared from a corselet of green velvet, representing the calix of a flower, and on her head there was the peduncle with its great arms of green velvet striped with diamonds. I don't know what species of quarrel Mistinguett tried to pick with me on the evening of the dressmakers' rehearsal; she pretended she could not wear this dress, which did not permit her to dance (she has worn many like it since); she raised innumerable difficulties with that obstinacy and disingenuousness which are the secret of the ladies of the theatre. The truth is that she had a contract, which obliged her to be dressed, on the stage as well as off it, by one of my former employees, whose name is unworthy of this book. I eliminated this robe, which would have produced a sensational effect, on which I had counted, from the scene, and I refused to make another out of it, for I felt myself incapable of doing better. Next day Mistinguett came on to the stage in the same dress she had criticised and refused the night before, but now her dress had been copied by the other house, from my model.

A great many words to devote to the telling of a piece of baseness, but it was necessary to tell it in order that the public may know to what disillusionment, to what bitterness, he who desires to create a little pure and healthy beauty in the dusty and corrupt atmosphere of the theatre or music hall must expose himself.

Mistinguett has always alleged that I am the only man who has ever made her afraid; she could not sustain my glance, for she was incapable of understanding what it contained. In her heart she preserved a secret hatred against me, and it was this feeling she found occasion to express on that day. I bear her no malice for it now.

Since I am telling my whole story, I must now relate that I assiduously followed the Quat' Z'Arts Ball, to which I was regularly invited. Nothing has ever seemed to me more charming than these libertine fêtes of youth, in which there is neither affectation nor pedantry. I remember especially an Assyrian evening, in the setting of the Moulin Rouge, which was one of the finest evocations of the past I have ever admired.

I had just dressed, for M. Rouché, a piece by Maurice Magre at the Theatre des Arts: it was called *Nabuchodonozor*. Segonzac had agreed to do the scenic decoration because I was doing the costumes, and we had been very amused at the rehearsals because it was de Max who was playing the part of *Nabuchodonozor*, and he was whimsical enough. He was on his hands and knees on the stage and was rehearsing that moment of the play when he had been changed into an ox. One of his favourite dancers arrived in a pirouette: it was the lovely Trouhanova who played this rôle, a rich and abundant nature. De Max, at the height of his delirium, ought to have cried out to her 'Butterfly! Butterfly!' But on one rehearsal night this cry did not come forth from his throat. The ox stopped playing and approaching on all fours the edge of the stage he called out, 'Rouché! Rouché! Tell me, old chap, aren't you afraid they will guy me? I say "Butterfly! Butterfly!" and you send me an elephant.'

De Max wore in that play the first theatrical costume I made. It was an immense cloak that I had had specially dyed to a tint which must have been that of the Tyrian purple. It was heightened with great strips of gold braid and on the head of the king changed into an ox there was set a monumental tiara, weighing thirteen pounds (but de Max was an artist who would submit to torture to produce the right effect). This tiara was conceived like a piece of goldsmith's work; it seemed as if sculpted in virgin gold, and was crowned with belfries, turrets and minarets. It was this costume I had borrowed to go to the Quat' Z'Arts Ball. A train of honour was attached to it, and drawn by a hundred women. It was a fine sight.

As a result of this appearance, I became the friend of the studios of the Ecole des Beaux-Arts, who asked me each year to participate in their fun, and to organise some sensational entry with the beautiful girls whom I had at my disposition. I always lent myself to their desires until the day when I was grossly received by a clumsy fool who marked me on the face with a brush full of green paint, to inform me, in the language of art-students, that I had passed the age of these rejoicings. I understood, and I never returned after, despite the insistence of some of my friends, and despite my incurable liking for all painters.

For I have always loved painters, and felt on an equal footing with them. It seems to me that we practise the same craft, and that they are my fellow workers.

At the period of which I am now telling I saw regularly two of them, both destined to a great future: Vlaminck and Derain. They lived in little hostelries by the water side at Chatou; I too. We lived there as did once the Impressionists and the friends of Caillebotte, at Argenteuil, in an atmosphere of healthy carefree liberty. I shall always remember Vlaminck's ferocious air and savage look, if one approached his canvas while he was working. He showed his pictures at a colour merchant's at the corner of the Pont de Rueil, and one of my friends used to say that when one went by in a car, pretty fast, they produced quite a good impression. He would not advance this proposition to-day, for Vlaminck has become a light of our time, and his talent is no longer arguable. One day I saw him, with Derain, moving. Mother Lefranc, the landlady, tired of giving them credit, had taken an extreme course, and thrown them out. I can still see them by the flowery banks, their boxes of colours under their arms, and their canvases in a wheelbarrow. What would Mme Lefranc not do to-day for these successful painters, if they still had a desire to return to her?

VII
The Faubourg
Saint Honoré

It was on a day in Mid-Lent that, wandering on foot in the fine *quartier* around the Champs Elysées, the Rue d'Artois, and the Avenue d'Antin (to-day the Avenue Victor Emmanuel III), I stopped in front of a waste piece of land closed in by a railing. It was a deserted property where, beneath vast and probably 100-year-old trees, the grass grew wild, chickens pecked about in every corner, and through the railings one could see all the cats of the quarter wandering in search of prey. The gate onto the road was closed, but I wanted to enter into this palace of the Sleeping Beauty, and I looked for a door.

There was one in the Faubourg Saint Honoré. A vault supported by columns gave access on to a courtyard closed in by an ancient building. It was the back of the hotel, whose magnificent façade looked upon the Avenue d'Antin. I persuaded the concierge to talk: The house had been abandoned for fifteen years. It had to be taken as a whole, and it was too big for a tradesman, while no private person wanted to repair these ruins, these fallen cornices, this roof that threatened to fall in.

Two days later I signed my lease. I undertook repairing works that lasted three months – they seemed interminable. I had the garden made like those I had seen at Versailles, and in the great châteaux of France. By the first of October the house was transformed: I had respected its august character, one would have thought it the residence of a grand seigneur of another day. An embroidered *parterre* spread out like a tapestry in the midst of the alleys: there was a lawn bristling with multi-coloured crocuses; there was a grassy amphitheatre leading to an airy room; there was a flight of three steps eighteen yards long, at whose extremity were two brazen hinds, light and leaping, two marvels I had brought back from Herculanum.

All those who lived an hour in this enchanted setting will be touched by these evocative details. One entered the house by ten doors giving upon the steps, and on summer days all the reception rooms could be opened like a gallery on to the garden. The carpets were of gooseberry red, and contrasted deliciously with the verdure of the *parterres*. Cunning chandeliers mingled in the perspective of mirrors their crystal stalactites. At the end of the principal salon a great square room, decorated with delicate frescoes, was the base of a grand formal staircase that had a beautiful old balustrade.

On the first floor there was the charming intimacy of the trying-on rooms, with chaise-longues, armchairs and couches, fine candelabra, and mirrors. It was in this enchanted and enchanting palace that, for fifteen years, all that was most subtle, Parisian and exotic in life paraded by.

On one side of the garden there rose the façade of a second house, where I had my personal quarters. It was there that I installed a marvellous statue I had bought from an importer of Chinese wares. It was the finest artistic object that ever left Eastern lands – a granite block representing a Bodhisatva: which may well have been the Goddess of Mercy, as was told me – unless it were not something altogether else. This statue was of such beauty that I wanted it to have, once more, a setting worthy of it; and I sacrificed a whole room on the ground floor of the house, giving on to my garden. I had the walls covered with a grey glaze, and lit by a single light, so that the goddess should find again the atmosphere she had known in the grottoes of Long-Nen or elsewhere, whence she had come.

I passed hours in consulting her in the troubled moments of my life, or I would contemplate her in her halo of light, which seemed to clothe her with all the prayers and desires of which she had been the object. How much human potentiality must have shattered itself against that impenetrable granite!

The six Chinese who had transported her on their shoulders to Pekin had been decapitated. She had been hidden for two years in the basements of the *wagon-lits* offices at Pekin, where she had waited for the momentary inattention of the Customs in order to escape from China. In my house she met the élite of France. Many artists and philosophers were introduced to her, and some thought themselves obliged to make definitive declarations before her, instead of confining themselves to admiration, and letting themselves be penetrated

by the metaphysical grandeur and eternal beauty she radiated. When
the war came, I shut her up with great care, convinced that, because
of her weight, nobody would attempt to steal her: and it was I who
brought her forth from her cave, when I sold her to the Metropolitan
Museum of New York. I go to see her on each of my journeys thither.
She occupies a place of honour in the circle of gods and goddesses of
the same epoch and the same origin. I do not think that she is, as I was
told, the statue of Mercy. I think rather that, if there is a Goddess of
Hypocrisy, it is she, for her expression is perfidious, and ill-luck came
into my house with her. I attribute to this goddess, who had cast an evil
spell over the six Chinese of Pekin, all the troubles that have assailed
me since I made her acquaintance. Need I add that on the very day
she entered New York, the United States decided to take part in the
Great War?

No indiscreet eye could penetrate my privacy. All my visitors uttered
the same exclamation: 'To have all this in the heart of Paris, what a
miracle!' People had said: 'You are too far away, you are out of the
movement of affairs, your clientèle will not follow you. Even the
tradesmen will refuse to deliver.' But I felt firmly that all that was
untrue, and that the Westward urge was irresistible. You must agree
that, since that epoch, this extreme point has been passed; the
Champs Elysées, which to-day are almost out-moded, have been taken
in their stride, and fashion laps the gates of the Bois de Boulogne.

The audacity of a dressmaker who openly and violently broke with
the traditions of the Rue de la Paix, and who deliberately put himself
afar from the Sacred Street, was not immediately understood. There
were arguments, there was much discussion at dinners and in clubs;
which all created a wave of curiosity, and this garden full of flowers,
that set the crown on my reputed enormous expenditure, excited the
criticism of the financiers. One month after the opening, my war had
been won. All Paris had come to me. From five o'clock to seven
o'clock there was a torrent. The most magnificent automobiles of the
capital daily performed their skilful evolutions around my *parterre*,
and all the women of elegance delighted to see my mannequins,
lissom as nymphs, file past in this living, colourful, but wholly unpre-
tentious scene. Every day eighty persons would ask me to let them see
the miracle of my gowns, flowering forth one by one, and I was forced

to confine the privilege of this spectacle to clients who had made up their minds to leave definite orders. This ostracism discontented some.

One day Baroness de —— summoned me to the telephone, to request me to send to her house, at two in the afternoon, my finest dresses and my most beautiful mannequins. I consented to give her this pleasure. Was she not the richest of my clients? And was I not the most complaisant of her purveyors?

A saleswoman left at the hour arranged, to accompany a squadron of pretty girls, and I urged them to be back quickly, in order not to miss the afternoon parade at the house. At half-past four I saw them return, heated, disordered, excited, and furious. 'Monsieur,' the saleswoman said to me, 'I must tell you what she has done to us, in order that you may write her a letter such as you know how to write. She made us parade in front of her gigolos, who made unpleasant comments, and who understood nothing at all about your dresses. Besides, they were only looking at the mannequins. As for her, she had an air of finding everything ridiculous, and she said to me, as we parted: 'I knew they were ugly, but I could not believe they were as ugly as all that!' You cannot tolerate that, Monsieur ... You must write to her, or to her husband.'

I had no resentment against the Baroness, and I replied to my saleswoman: 'Don't worry; surefooted vengeance will come: we must have no scandal!'

A little after that, the crowd still continuing to flow to my house, the saleswoman came to seek me in my office, and grinning all over, said: 'Monsieur, guess who is there? Baroness ——. This time you are not going to miss your chance, I trust?' My face lit up. I licked my lips. I rubbed my hands together, like a mongoose about to kill a snake, and gaily I descended my staircase. All the seats in my salon were occupied; there were even some women crouched on cushions. There reigned the deep, concentrated silence of solemn hours. I went up to the Baroness, and greeted her:

'Madame,' I said, 'I know that my dresses do not please you, you informed my saleswoman of this in your house, where I have already received an affront. I do not wish to suffer another in my own house, and I ask you to depart.'

I saw rage rise from her heart to her face.

'Monsieur,' she said to me, 'do you know to whom you are speaking?'

'It is precisely because I know, Madame, that I express myself as I do. Kindly withdraw.'

'I am not accustomed to be put out of the house by my purveyors, and I will not go.'

'Madame, I no longer consider myself one of your purveyors. However, if you insist on staying here, my dresses will not be shown to you.'

And turning towards the audience, I added:

'Those who wish to see my models are requested to go up to the first floor, where the parade will continue.'

The Baroness stood up, and with flaming eyes uttered these words: 'You will hear from me . . .'

Then she left precipitately.

On the following morning I was with my heads of departments in the glass-walled office whence I dominated all the activities of my house, and which opened on to all its organs. Every morning we had a report and conference, as is customary.

The Baroness's saleswoman entered like a hurricane.

'Monsieur, do you know who is there? It is Baron de ——; Monsieur, do not go, he will do you some injury . . .'

I went down at once in order not to keep him waiting, and I presented myself to him.

'You are Monsieur Paul Poiret?' he asked me in an even voice.

'Yes, Monsieur.'

'It is you, isn't it, who put my wife out of your house yesterday?'

'Yes, Monsieur.'

My assurance pleased him, he seemed to reflect, his face lit with a smile, and he said to me gently:

'You have done well. I know someone who adores your dresses, but who did not want to meet her . . .'

And he departed . . .

No later than the next morning I received a visit from a lady who was to become one of my most faithful clients.

I did not wait for my success to grow by itself. I worked like a demon to increase it, and everything that could stimulate it seemed good to me. In Paris I was the height of fashion; I wanted to force the attention of Europe and the whole world. I organised a colossal enterprise, which consisted in making the tour of the chief capitals of Europe accompanied by nine mannequins. When I think to-day of the difficulty of realising this programme, I know not if I would still have the strength to undertake it. For it was not only a question of leading forth nine mannequins, but of bringing them back to Paris safe and sound. I did not wish to give the impression of a Barnum carting around prodigies, nor of a music-hall impresario. My tour had to keep an air of distinction, and my propaganda depended upon the good manners and deportment of these young ladies.

Two automobiles carried the travellers. All the mannequins wore the like costume. It was a very Parisian uniform, composed of a blue serge tailor-made and a comfortable cloak in reversible beige plaid. On their heads they wore oilcloth hats with an embroidered P. It was extremely chic. The secretary-general of the tour travelled by rail with the dresses, preceding us in the towns, and seeing to accommodation at hotels. He had to take precautions in order that the group of rooms devoted to the personnel should be inaccessible to the profane, and easily watched over. Usually he occupied one side at the end of the corridor, and I the other, to make a barrage against the importunate.

We had, none the less, certain difficult hours, notably at St. Petersburg, where the gilded youth showed itself particularly audacious and enflamed. The florists and confectioners must have had colossal receipts on those days, but nothing passed, neither flowers, nor bonbons, nor billet-doux, nor banknotes. We were working for the honour of my house, and it was incompatible with such liberties. I finished by getting my entourage to admit it.

No incident marked our passage at Frankfurt or Berlin, except a public curiosity that rose after us like a gale. At Warsaw we were pounced upon by the Russian Customs, and I lost two days in opening my baggage in all the bureaux, where I tried to prove that it was not a question of merchandise but of costumes intended to be shown as a spectacle. They pretended not to understand me. The introductions I had brought with me were useless. I was to be seen running about in the station, from one office to another, calling for help to prevent the Customs men unpacking with their dirty hands the new stockings, the fragile veilings, the light gloves. They took a malicious pleasure in handling it all, and I began to be seriously upset when an unknown traveller took pity on me. 'Will you allow me to see to it?' he said, when he saw my distress; and taking from his case two notes of 100 roubles each, he showed them to the Customs men. I do not know what then happened. But no longer did any of my goods spread about the counters, the trunks were closed, loaded on to a carriage, and directed to my hotel. I received smiles and courtesy from all my adversaries, now become my friends. I had made the acquaintance of the Russian Administration.

From Warsaw we went to Moscow. It was in November and there was snow everywhere, though the weather was fine, and the carriages were odiously overheated (we had to take the train, for the automobiles could not travel over the roads, and awaited us in Bucarest). We took our places in two compartments. There was scarcely anyone in this *train de luxe,* and in the whole corridor there were only ourselves, and a couple called Lazareff. M. Lazareff had a stentorian voice, that dominated the roar of the train. A few minutes after the departure my girls went down like a house of cards beneath the stifling heat. I opened the window in the compartment – there were two to each door, and the second was sealed. I broke it to allow my people to breathe. M. Lazareff, thundering out, complained that this made a draught in his compartment, and obtained the support of the guard. The latter came and complained to me, perceived that I had broken the seal, put in another, and expressed to me in Russian exactly what he thought of my conduct. As the heat was intolerable, and I saw all my people visibly withering, I took the bronze ash tray, which is an institution in the *wagon-lits* of the whole world, and I broke the second window, to get a little air. It is this need for air that makes fish leap out of the water. But on our arrival in Moscow, I was netted when I left my compartment by a squadron of *gendarmes,* who had been informed by telephone: and the journalists who awaited me with their cameras were enabled to photograph me in the middle of this escort.

I cannot pass over Moscow without halting my memories a moment in the house of Mme Lamanoff, who was one of the great dress designers of those good days, and a friend whom I shall always keep in pious memory. She revealed to me the whole phantasmagoria of that half Eastern life which is Moscow, – I still see it, the ikons, the Kremlin, the bell turrets of St. Basil's, the Iswolchtnitks, the monstrous sturgeon, the iced caviar, the marvellous collection of modern pictures belonging to M. Tchoukine, and the *soirées* at Yarhe's. May Mme Lamanoff, now buried beneath the ashes and lava of the political cataclysm, find here, and her husband also, the warmest expression of the friendship and gratitude owed her by Tout-Paris.

I still remember how astonished I was to be able to communicate by telephone, in one minute, from Moscow with St. Petersburg (for that was then its name), whither I went next day to give a lecture and a demonstration.

The demonstration took place. It was given in each European capital for the benefit of those charitable enterprises that were patronised by the greatest ladies; in Vienna the Arch Duchesses, in Petrograd the Grand Duchesses, who assured its success, in order to raise contributions for their work. When I went to the Petrograd Theatre I was struck by the number of crosses in red chalk to be seen on the seats that were for hire, and I congratulated the box office man on his energy. He replied that these signs did not indicate the seats that had been booked, but places reserved for the police. The greater the number of exalted personages in the theatre, the greater the number of these seats. The first rows of the orchestra had been removed in order to install gilded armchairs sent from the Court, in which alone the most august behinds were allowed to sit, and I was astonished, half an hour before the beginning of the show, to see soldiers come in armed with a probe like that of Customs men, with which they examined the padding of the armchairs to assure themselves that they contained no bombs nor other murderous engines. This was in 1912.

All these precautions were sound, for revolutionaries were at that time everywhere, and even my mannequins were suspected, since they might, from the stage, have attempted some outrage. To assure himself that their attire did not hide in its folds any infernal machine the Chief of Police, in full uniform, spent the whole evening in their dressing room. Paulette came to me, and complained of his embarrassing presence, and I tried to explain to him, but he declined to depart. When the parade was finished I asked Paulette to give him two roubles as a tip; she put them discreetly in his hand: he accepted them without the flicker of an eye.

I was positively disgusted by my visit to St. Petersburg, for what one could see of Russia at that time threw a light on the probable value of her promises. When I returned to Paris I advised my family to sell everything they had left in Russian securities, and I told them what I thought of this worm-eaten Government, which was incapable of resisting the pressure of the people. My mother answered me that there was nothing to fear, and that if a new régime should come to pass, its first care would be to recognise the engagements entered into by preceding Governments. Such is the value of experience.

On leaving St. Petersburg I went to Bucarest, where I lived in the Hotel Boulevard. On the evening of our arrival all the carriages of the dandies were drawn up in front of the hotel, and awaited my demoiselles to take them for a promenade. I had to decide that they should not go out, and I made myself unpopular with these messieurs. Did not our own private cars await us, and had not our chauffeurs more than one advantage over these Bucarest drivers, whose fluted voices and lamentable histories astounded my troupe?

I could say with Figaro: 'Welcomed in one town, imprisoned in the next and everywhere superior to events.' For, on arriving in Budapest, I had the surprise of being arrested! I was led to the Chief of Police, who asked me a thousand questions as to the object of my journey, and explained to me that, not having taken out a licence, I could not give any demonstration liable to injure local trade, or compete with the efforts of the autochthonous dress designers. One of the local newspapers having taken up my cause, the town was divided into two camps, and my enterprise profited from the publicity born of controversy.

I still have friends in Budapest with whom I laugh over these vicissitudes. Did not one of them take into his head the notion of making my mannequins believe that the river which bathes this lovely town, and runs beneath its ancient bridges, was none other than the Hunyadi Janos, celebrated for the laxative virtue of its water, whose benefits they could experience by leaving the windows of their rooms open to the mists of night! And, accompanied by his friends, he came one evening to serenade them with mandolines.

Whatever the charms of travel, one is always happy to return to one's own home: we stamped with impatience in Vienna and Munich, we burned to find once more, in Paris, a public of connoisseurs more enlightened than anywhere else in the world. We arrived at the German frontier at lunch time, all the troupe were famished, we had to have a meal in the cars themselves. An authentic Strasbourg *pâté de foie gras* was devoured on the spot, washed down with two bottles of Pol Roger. We smelled our home stables; I could no longer make myself the master of their impatience, which is what must excuse the excesses that followed. Those who have travelled for two months with one little French girl can imagine what it is to have to manage nine!

Our cars had been drawn up at the side of the road, and perpendicular to it, so that the bonnets encroached slightly upon the lines of the steam tramway. When the tram arrived, it had to stop a few yards from our vehicles, and the conductor descended to request us to give him room to pass; he did it in such terms, and with such violent and exasperating mimicry, that he excited howls of laughter from all the delinquents; furious, and beside himself at being unable to make himself understood, for he only spoke German, he made as if to climb on to one of the cars and drive it himself. Then passions rose to a height, and the affair threatened to turn serious. Everyone saw red; I had to request the chauffeurs, very gently, to move their cars a little in order to facilitate the passage of the tram. It continued its course, and we too. When we arrived at the Bridge of Kehl we were hemmed in by an altogether impressive barrage of police, warned by telephone by the tram conductor, whose rage must have increased steadily. We were all taken to the police station, and there I asked for an interpreter, for whom we had to wait a considerable time. The girls, whose mad laughter could not be controlled, wanted to know the resources of the place, and disappeared one by one.

When the interpreter and the Police Commissary had come, I showed my papers and explained the incident.

The Commissary, perceiving from the newspaper cuttings with whom he was dealing, and reading that I had been received at Potsdam by the family of the Emperor, showed himself full of deference and courtesy. We were immediately released, and it was only then that I became aware of all that had happened, for my mannequins showed me that they had set hands on all the seals and stamps they could find in the office of the Commissary. In vain I painted to them the face of this unhappy functionary, deprived of his tools and materials, unable to sign permits and documents. I obtained only laughter, and I was forced to be content with it. After all, we had passed the Bridge of Kehl, and I had no desire to return to the other side; but now that I have told the truth about this story, I wonder how I should be received, if I were ever to return there?

VIII
My Amusements

Someone some day will write the history of the Mortigny Club, for I cannot believe that so characteristic and vivid an element of the history of my generation will be allowed to be lost to mind. It was an intimate club where one could see more or less well-known artists intermingled with figures of the great world belonging to divers societies. M. L. Allez, M. Hamelle, General Oznobitchine (Military Attaché to the Russian Embassy), Colonel Bentley Mott (Military Attaché to the American Embassy) and a handful of Grand Dukes, Boris, Cyril, and others.

One day a Revolutionary Ball was given there, and I saw the painter Eschmann tap the Grand Duke Cyril familiarly on the nape of the neck; the latter was wearing a Court costume, and Eschmann said:

'A fine head to cut off, Monseigneur.'

That shows the sort of jolly familiarity that reigned.

One day Eschmann was on M. Hamelle's yacht in Brittany, and when he had just pulled in a superb mackerel he said to his host:

'Do you know what a fish like this may be worth in Paris?'

M. Hamelle answered him:

'I am not accustomed to do my marketing myself, but I imagine chez Prunier it would be worth three francs fifty.'

Then Eschmann, placing the fish in a newspaper, presented it to him, saying:

'Monsieur Hamelle, I now have, at last, the opportunity and the pleasure of returning to you, at a single stroke, all the courtesies you have shown me.'

And there was also Forain, whom all Paris knows, loves or fears. The portrait of Forain? If the devil became a hermit, and if he chose for his incarnation the appearance of a sacristan, he would resemble Forain. He would have that mouth, both laughing and venomous, whose grin is always chewing upon a perpetual sarcasm. The most sardonic caricaturist of our epoch, famous for the drawings he did for the *Figaro*, which are as mordant in their line as in their captions, Forain is a man of the first importance, of whom account must be taken when the history of our times comes to be written.

I will not go back to the epoch when he played a political rôle in the Dreyfus affair, by his direction of a famous anti-Dreyfusard paper. I met him later and I saw him, above all, at the Mortigny, where he kept himself bright by contact with youth. He has always been known to have a ferocious wit, and dangerously sharpened claws.

I sometimes saw him in the summer, at the period when men are alone and with very little to do in Paris; we lunched together, and he plied me with savoury stories and anecdotes.

One day especially, when we were lunching chez Larue, he presented me to Manzi, who was his picture dealer. It will be remembered that, following the Dreyfus affair, the Jewish picture dealers had thrown all Forain's works on to the market, and put them up for sale at ridiculous prices, to ruin the master's value and lose him all estimation. They had counted without the astuteness of one of themselves, who was Manzi. The latter bought up all his work at prices around five francs each, and composed the finest collection of Forains that could then be had. After things had calmed down, he had a show: it was a resounding success, and he made an immense profit out of it. Forain thus presented him to me on that occasion:

'Here is Manzi, the only Jew who has ever got the better of the Bernheims.'

Another time, at Prunier's, a little while after the death of Edwards, he told me various stories about this strange chap of an editor. – He had never been able to get on with his father, Forain said, 'And at his funeral, as he was walking behind the hearse, I know someone who said, "That is the first time they have been seen going out together."'

Then he told me other stories about Edwards, and about Edwards' father, who, he said, had been a dentist to the pashas of Turkey; as these gentry did not like pain, he had made a large fortune by introducing the use of cocaine, whose discovery was recent. The women were no less cowardly than the men, wherefore he had also treated the harems and, taking advantage of his access, he had sold authentic champagne to these ladies, who were very fond of it. But the

Koran prohibited the importation of wines into Turkey. He therefore had many difficulties in purveying it, and found a way through them by delivering his champagne – sugared liquor of the third class – in surgical syringes, of a kind much used in Turkey, instead of in bottles. Such was the origin of Edwards' fortune, according to Forain. He was so amusing as he told these stories that our neighbours at table had stopped reading their papers and strained their ears to catch it all. He was not insensible to the plaudits of the gallery, and he deployed all his resources.

Since I am speaking of the Mortigny and of Forain, it would be unforgivable if I did not recall the touching memory left by Abel Truchet, whose goodness equalled Forain's cruelty. Truchet, whose beginnings had been very hard, had retained from them a charming good fellowship. He was sentimental and tender, sometimes showing his teeth and imagining he thus gave himself a wicked air, but in reality only masking the tremors of his sensitiveness. He had done a favour to everyone in the world, and wearied all his connections to procure help for one and money for another; he was a skilled and politic schemer at the time when the picture salons distributed their medals and prizes. I have two stories to tell about him which will describe better than a portrait Abel Truchet's physiognomy.

One morning he was to be seen, with his pointed beard and his art student's hat, installing his easel by the borders of the Odet, at Quimper. When he began to work some little boys dared one another, and drew near him, and began to annoy him. There were several of them, of differing appearance. One, especially, was rosy cheeked and very blonde, and so charming that two old ladies passing by summoned him, called him 'Little Jesus,' and gave him a penny. Truchet, who had looked on at this scene, chose out the most hairy and ugly of the band, and giving him two pennies, said with tears in his eyes: 'Now, you there, go and blow your nose.' And he said to his wife, who was with him: 'That one is too ugly for anybody ever to give him anything.'

For Julia, his wife, generally worked beside him, and shared his artist's joys. One day when he was painting in Venice, in front of Santa Maria della Salute, everything was going well, the effect he wanted was coming easily, he was squashing his tubes on his palette with intoxication and, in a moment of expansion, turning to Julia, he said to her: 'Believe me, one would pay money to work at this trade.'

As well as those of whom I have already spoken, there were many of the Mortignys who deserve a portrait, but I do not want to cut the ground from beneath the feet of my friend Bain, who owes it to the club to write its amusing history, one day.

When I felt that fortune was smiling on me and that I was upheld by a silver wave, I allowed myself to indulge a bit more extensively in my sports and pleasures. I loved boats; my friends, the Monnot brothers, had inculcated in me a taste for sailing from the time they had made my acquaintance at Doucet's. They had taken me along to the Chatou Sailing Club, of which I, like them, was a pillar. It was an amiable society of young yachtsmen, whose taste for sport did not exclude that for the social arts. Amongst them there reigned a perfect jolliness and good fellowship that delighted me. I fled to Chatou whenever I could get away to rest. Memories and mementoes of our great predecessors were still to be found there: Maupassant, Renoir, Sisley, Monet, Pissaro, Caillebote and Caran d'Ache, who had all frequented 'The Froggery' and the Fournaise dock. Monnot knew more than one piquant story about them, and it was our pleasure to get those who had known them to talk, especially a carpenter of ill repute called Langlais, who was the funniest of funnies.

I had gone down the Seine several times in a sailing boat. We used to go by short stages from Chatou to Havre, stopping in the pleasantest bits of greenness for meals or sleep, for we slept in the boat. I wrote an account of one of these cruises for a yachting paper, in verse.[1]

At the period of which I am speaking I permitted myself the pleasure of a houseboat; I had it built at Maisons-Laffitte, with the advice of Louis Sue, who was a good architect and a delightful friend. He took part in my first cruise, which was not what a vain people would suppose, for we left Maisons-Laffitte for Brittany, and we moored in a little port near Lorient. It is necessary that I should give some explanation of this phenomenon: we went up the Seine as far as

[1]Translator's note: Very detailed and very amusing rhymes – too difficult to translate.

Saint-Mammès – we were towed by a boat I had had brought from Arcachon, of the sort called a pinnace; neither of the two boats drew more than 30 centimetres, so that we could land anywhere. At Saint-Mammès we took the canal to Orleans, and behold, we were in the Loire which, precisely in that year, was navigable. I took a pilot, for one has to know this river very well to adventure on it, and we descended by short stages, stopping wherever it seemed good to us. Never was voyage more restful. I played the accordion on the boat, abandoning myself to contemplation of the long screens of poplars bordering the monotonous but always laughing, and charmingly intimate, canals. Our stores were replenished with wine when we came to the purlieus of Chinon, Bourgueil and Vouvray. Then it was the turn of the slopes of Saumur and Anjou, and of Muscadet at Oudon, so that of a truth our vessel was well ballasted when we arrived at Nantes.

France is so rich in good things that one can everywhere take samples of gastronomic specialities; the fattened pullets of Le Mans, the potted pork of Tours, the forcemeat of Vouvray, etc. . . .

We entered the Nantes canal at Brest, then, via Blavet, we came down to Port-Louis; there I waited for fine weather and, one day before dawn, I weighed anchor to take to sea, in a dead calm that mirrored the moonlight. I penetrated into all the little creeks of Brittany that opened to starboard.

Quimperle river opened to me its enchanted estuary, then came Pouldu, then the port of Douëllan, and I stopped in the most beautiful corner of Brittany, which is unknown to any traveller, and has never known a motor car. There I passed happy holidays. I had with me a sailing boat, and I went fishing; I had my cook from Paris, who treated ravishingly everything I brought her. It was a land of Cocaigne.

Segonzac, Boussingault, Sue, Max Jacob, all my friends knew this boat, which was called *The Nomad*, and they shared my holidays in it. In the evening after a good dinner, we talked long about the fine arts and literature, in front of us choice Calvados and Marcs, and we consolidated our ideas and opinions about beauty. But . . . I have always been surprised to see how lazy painters are, and how reluctant to take up their brushes, and I was astonished at the littleness of their activity, and the very small hurry they seemed to be in to actualise their talent. It seemed to me that if I had had their powers and knowledge,

I would have covered the doors and the panels of the walls with representations of nature. What ardour I had at that time, what a need to work and produce! I have never seen anybody who equalled me in this respect.

At night I used to see the fishing boats with their great brown sails glide past me and, silently, make for the open sea. Sometimes I went out with the fishermen. One fine morning, when the wind was favourable, I prepared my own boat, and made sail toward the isle of Groix. On the way I was literally surrounded by a multitude of sea birds. It was as if in an aviary. My sailor told me that we were over a fish bank and, in fact, when we had dropped our lines into the water, I took a hundred mackerel from the waves in half an hour. When we arrived at Groix a squall came up, and I perceived that we should be unable to return that day. I asked my sailor if he had any money. He had not, nor had I, since we had started out in a hurry. Nevertheless, we had to pass the night on the isle. I put all my fish into a basket, and went to sell it from door to door. On the following day I decided to return, but the tempest still raged, and I was dismasted outside Pouldu. It is memories like this, full of health and nature, which, in my opinion, give the most fragrant perfume to the days of my youth. You must forgive me for letting myself dwell on them.

When the fine weather was over, I left my boat in Brittany, and sometimes I came back in the winter to pass one, two or three days with my friends, and to shoot a few sea birds. I came back from these flights to offer the spoils of the chase to my employees' refectory, for with them I maintained a close camaraderie. I had a great affection for my workers, and I had no thought but of how to improve their situation. When I was in America I studied with interest everything that the industrialists of the great cities there are experimenting with to help their humble collaborators. There are baths, rest rooms, libraries, dance halls, phonographs and rocking chairs on the roofs of the buildings, during the hours of sunshine. I had dreamed of adapting all this progress and these innovations for the personnel of a great Paris house. But it was not long before I perceived that Parisian working women scarcely appreciate an employer's benefactions. They love nothing so much as freedom, and one cannot please them save by giving them the key to the wide world. To colour their cheeks with a little rouge, put a scarf round their throats, a little cloche on their heads, and a gamp under their arms, THAT is the familiar liberating rite which enchants them more than anything in the world.

To come back to my travels, I must recount the voyage I made in 1910 (the more I stir up my memories, the more astonished I am that I was able to realise so many projects in so short a time). I had hired a great yacht in the port of Marseilles, it was a steam yacht, the *Henriette*, that belonged to M. de Neuville, a banker. Its displacement was 400 tons, it was 70 metres long, and had a crew of fifteen. I resolved to undertake a cruise in the Mediterranean, and invited a few friends to accompany me. They were from the Mortigny Club, Berquin, Jourdain, Lièvre, Boussingault, and Segonzac, all painters. Also, my friend Brown, who adored navigation.

This boat, that had seemed enormous in the port of Marseilles, was not so important out at sea. It rolled frightfully, and shipped water forward. Wherefore I passed my nights on the watch, while my comrades, who had put their lives into my hands, slept in all confidence. Furthermore I had every imaginable tribulation with the crew. I had not taken the precaution of seeing that they were properly dressed. That seemed to me so obvious. From the first day out I was surprised to see my men wearing buttoned boots and little chestnut jackets. Respectful of the traditions of yachting, I liked to have everything brightly spick and span on board. Nothing seems to me finer than the discipline and orderliness of sailors. So I had the whole lot properly dressed, and insisted upon correctness. But the captain himself gave the signal for anarchy on the day he appeared on the bridge wrapped in a woollen shawl, and wearing on his head an Alpine cap his Penelope must have knitted him before he left.

Our first call was at Ajaccio. There the chief cook, drunk as a Corsican fiddler, climbed on to the bridge cutlass in hand, announcing that he would kill the first man to approach him. I approached him with a thousand precautions, and talking friendlily with him I got him ashore over the drawbridge; and as soon as we had reached dry land, I ordered the bridge to be drawn into the ship. Thus he was effectively disembarked. I told the Consul, and engaged another cook. Everywhere we went I had to bear tribulations of this kind, either when we were taking on stores, or with the men, and while my friends visited the towns, I spent my time at marine outfitters occupied in every kind of negotiation and formality. When I returned I swore an oath that if ever I went on another cruise it would be in the capacity of an invited guest. None the less, we passed six exquisite weeks in the Mediterranean, visiting Naples, Amalfi, Pestum, Sicily, Kairouan, Tunis, Bougie, Constantine, Algiers, Oran, Almería, Alicante, Valencia, Tarragona, and Barcelona, and it was with regret that we abandoned our white ducks and yachting caps.

I could not detach myself from the society of my friends, who maintained in me a beneficent state of mind by their perpetual gaiety and their admirable independence, but I had the continual disillusionment of seeing them so little in love with their craft that they could resist for two and a half months the temptation of taking up their brushes to make a sketch – and in the face of so many things deserving to be set down. Not one of my comrades felt the need of painting during the whole cruise. It really shocked me, and it was I who one day took my palette and in two hours executed a portrait of my friend Brown, in the blue calm near Sorrento. He played the accordion while I painted him . . .

What I had seen of Arab lands commanded me imperiously to return to them. I felt within me an Oriental soul, and I could not resist the attraction of these lands of the sun. I was to return to them immediately after the war.

IX
The High Art of Dressmaking

This chapter will be an elementary course in *La Grande Couture*:

The personnel of a great dressmaking house is composed of several categories of employees: First of all, there are the technicians, that is to say, the triers-out and the *premières*, and their workwomen. It is they who execute the models, under the inspiration of the designers. They are the executives of the intentions of the creator, they must assimilate them, and give them an impeccable form. For one cannot, indeed, conceive of a *nouveauté* that should not have been perfectly tried out, of an innovation that should sin through any technical defect.

In a great house a *première* earns, on an average 60,000 francs a year, and ought to have, in my view, a certain degree of culture. If her means of existence do not allow her to live in a certain ease, she is incapable of understanding the subtleties and refinements of the designer who, himself, is by definition an artist in luxury.

I have had good *premières*, who knew their trade perfectly and were valiant workers, but who lacked this understanding and assimilation of the intentions and phantasies of the inventor. For instance: Antoinette, whom one day I advised to take a lover, for her inexperience prevented her from appreciating the sensuous charm which is the very expression of a dress. To the profane it may seem astonishing that this consideration should play a rôle in estimating the value of a commercial employee. Nevertheless, in my opinion it is an irrefutable principle so far as dressmaking is concerned that employees whose senses are not cultivated can only play a limited rôle. It is possible that Paris is the city where all the light fantasias of fashion flourish precisely because Paris is the city where the life of the senses flowers most freely.

A good *première* must sense the significance and the detail of an *ensemble*. For subtle personalities, who have reached a certain degree of emotional and intellectual evolution, in a dress as in a picture there is only one point where it is possible to place a spot of colour. It could not satisfy there, or there; it is *here* that it must be put. It is a sort of need or instinct that one satisfies and slakes by pinning on the particular detail of decoration at the precise place where it ought to be. All those who have devoted themselves to the art, or better, to the science of Cubism, or simply to composition, have established that there is a secret geometry which is the key of æsthetic satisfaction. What is true of line and volume is true of colour and its values. Generally women do possess this innate, and further perfectible, instinct, which permits them to judge whether a detail is in its right place, and whether it has the importance and the tint required. A *première* lacking this essential gift isn't worth anything.

But she must also thoroughly understand her profession, in order to have an ascendancy over her clients, and inspire them with confidence instantly and once for all. Furthermore, she must possess great sweetness of character, and angelic patience. I am incapable of describing certain scenes that take place in the fitting rooms of some houses I know, where the clients, tired out by long-continued standing, become nervous, weep, and sometimes even tear their dresses in fury. Often my appearance has put an end to a crisis of this kind. There are two schools: either I would arrive in the Salon with that infinite calm that has always served me, and I would say to the exasperated client: 'Madame, be calm, probably you made a mistake when you gave your order; your dress does not satisfy you, I don't want you to make yourself ill over a trifle, leave it. Let us not speak of it further. I will make a pretty cushion out of it, and for you, we will make something else, whatever you want. Don't look at it, since the sight of it wounds you. We will take it right away.' At this point it would sometimes happen that the lovely client, now tranquillised, would conceive a fresh desire for her dress, and become attached to it. On other occasions, according to the nature of the case, I would be implacable, and I would say, 'Madame, you came to Poiret knowing that Poiret is the first house in the world. Very well then, Poiret is me, and I, Poiret, I tell you: this dress is good, it is beautiful, and it suits you. If you don't like it, so much the worse, take it away, but I will never make you another. Our minds are not of a sort to understand one another.' This argument, too, had its value and efficacy.

Then come the saleswomen, who by definition are sellers, and but seldom connoisseurs. Very few of them influence the taste of their customers, or exercise any direction over their choice. Generally they have to deal with women who have made a long study of their seductive resources, and who know themselves well enough to understand what becomes them. A Parisienne, especially, never adopts a model without making in it changes of capital importance, and particularising it to suit herself. An American woman chooses the model presented to her, and buys it just as it is, while a Parisienne wants it to be blue if it is green, or garnet if it is blue, and adds a fur collar, and changes the sleeves, and suppresses the bottom buttons. It was M. Patou who first asserted that the future of *La Grande Couture* lay in ready-made clothes. He was speaking for himself, and his own interests, for this point of view is heretical, and presupposes a certain ignorance of creative dress designing. The high art of dressmaking consists precisely in developing the individuality of each woman. The model can only be used as a means of suggestion, and not of subjection. There ought to be as many models as there are women. Wherefore the rôle of the ideal saleswoman consists in composing on the theme of the model numberless variations, one for each client.

But there are few indeed who carry out their work in consciousness of such qualifications. Excited by rivalry, and the desire to realise a big total figure and make her commission, each of them tries to effect a great number of sales, and effects them badly.

A third category of employees is that engaged in management and in buying, that is to say in purchasing and receiving stuffs, embroideries, mercery, buttons; estimating and measuring materials for use, and giving out to the workshops all the ingredients necessary for the fulfilment of an order. A good buyer must know Paris and its resources of every sort, must know the speciality of each wholesaler and his capabilities and resources, and must be able to procure without delay everything she is asked; she must also have a good eye for nuances of colour, and be possessed of irreproachable integrity.

Those are the three essential elements of a dressmaking house. All the rest belongs to the artistic domain, and now I want to speak of the mannequins.

The word is very ill chosen. A mannequin is not that wooden instrument, unprovided with head or heart, on which robes are hung as on a clothes hanger. The living mannequin, who was invented by the great Worth, the first of the name, the pioneer of the industry of *la grande couture*, proves that the wooden mannequin did not fulfil the need. The living mannequin is a woman who must be more feminine than all other women. She must react beneath a model, in spirit soar in front of the idea that is being born from her own form, and by her gestures and pose, by the entire expression of her body, she must aid the laborious genesis of the new creation.

I have had many mannequins, and very few who were worthy of their priestesshood. Perhaps they never had an idea of the rôle they could have played in the flowering forth of my thought. I remember one of them who was called Andrée. She was stupid as a goose, but beautiful as a peacock. If I said to her in the morning: 'Andrée, you are the most beautiful of all my women,' her smile would broaden so that one could see her dazzling teeth. She was like an anemone expanding in the sea under the influence of a genial current. She would palpitate and dilate for the whole day: she would spread out her peacock's tail. On those days she appeared in my salons like a Messalina, like an Indian queen, with majestic and haughty pretension, and her sovereign carriage made the authentic princesses, before whom she stalked, ponder deeply. I saw more than one duke bite the head of his stick to put himself in countenance, and insert his monocle the better to observe her. Alas, what painful surprise, what disillusionment she would have caused!

Yvette was one of my stars. She was a little Parisienne from Batignolles, with a voice like a penny whistle. Fortunately her duties did not oblige her to speak. She was lively and joyous, with a great mouth that was always smiling, and such intelligent eyes that they lit up everything put on her back. She had taste, and understood or divined everything one wanted to express through her, and could foresee my intention, and lent herself to the execution of a new movement with subtle intelligence. I am not astonished that she showed herself cruel to a gallant Ambassador.

Paulette was for a long time the one I preferred, because she responded best to the sort of dresses I was then designing, perhaps precisely because she inspired me with them. She was a vaporous blonde, whose pale blue eyes seemed made of porcelain or of glass. With round arms and rounded shoulders she was plump and elegantly rolled as a cigarette. How comely, and how French! One day I made for her a *Bastille* costume, in striped red and white muslin, with a tri-coloured cockade. She would indeed have made all the gates of a prison burst open. Another time she wore a Scots dress, with a little vest of black velvet and a béret, of which all Scotsmen of the 42d degree would have been jealous. The way in which she gave life to everything I put on her could really be called collaboration, and that is precisely what I wanted to say at the beginning of this nomenclature: the mannequin must assimilate the spirit of her costume, and act its personality, and put on its significance. Beneath Paulette's angelic appearance, and her pale blue eye, there was hidden a malice, and perhaps a viciousness, whose depths I never learned. I have said that I had an office whence I was able to plunge my eye into the activities of all my departments. It was thanks to this that one day I saw my Paulette give her companions, gathered as if in a class, a delicate course in love.

I must mention also little Andrée, a blonde miniature of a woman, a small scale Pompadour.

Simone, grave and reserved, was like a nun, who with sly eye should discover in a mirror all the effects of her garment, the better to underline and emphasise them.

But for a few who interested themselves in the work, how many did I find who, taking no share in the dread terrors of creation, lent the presence of their bodies with indifference? Those truly deserve to be called by the wretched name of mannequin.

I have not spoken of the bookkeepers, for they are more or less the same in every trade, that is to say, monotonous, narrow, and unimaginative, unaware of the way in which one must treat a certain class of client and impatient to set hands on their accounts, arguing about everything, incapable of making a business live, but skilled in plunging it into lethargy and anæsthetising it by compressing its vital organs. I have only known one administrator really worthy of the name: my faithful Rousseau, to whom I render profound homage. He entered my service at a salary of 500 francs a month, doubting whether he could be of service to me. A modest but devoted worker, he soon learned the mechanism of this trade that was new to him. He controlled its play, and in a very short time he knew exactly where results – which he enhanced magnificently – could be achieved. He exercised a gentle surveillance over the workers, an equable pressure on each person's effort, a continuous examination of the sales, and a systematic check on the purchases: and he made the net profits under his régime rise to 42 per cent, at a period which was beginning to be difficult (1911). More, he was a charming friend, paternal and affectionate, with whom I worked like a brother. He never refused me the sums I asked to satisfy my caprices. If I wanted to give a costly fête, or carry out some fantastic scheme, I would approach him and confide my whim. 'Ah, ah,' he would say, 'I see you coming. This is going to cost us dear again.' Then I would look at him sideways and say: 'It is a little matter of a hundred thousand.' 'You can have them,' he would reply to me with a grimace, 'but don't get accustomed to it.' One could do something, before the war, with a hundred thousand francs.

It was thus that Rousseau tolerated and aided my follies. I must add that I always gave way, with pleasure, to his objurgations. How good life was with him, and how good was work!

I was with him in my office when one morning I saw arrive M. Coty, small, douce, laced into a pale grey suit, with a little straw hat on his head. I did not know him. A song of my youth came to my lips:

> *He was a little man*
> *All dressed in grey*
> *Hey, hey . . .*

He seated himself with assurance in an armchair and made me the following declaration:

'I have come to buy your perfumery business.'

'But,' I told him, 'it is not for sale.'

'If you continue as you are doing,' he answered, 'you will take fifteen years before you reach any great importance. If you come with me, you will profit from my management, and in two years you will be worth as much as I am.'

'Quite so, but in two years my business would be yours, while in the contrary case, in fifteen years it would still be my own property.'

'You understand nothing about business, Monsieur,' he replied, rising brusquely, and squashing his boater on his little head, he departed raging.

Silently we watched him go; M. Coty had the dimensions of Bonaparte.

X
The Decorative Arts

I have often travelled in Germany. I was first attracted there by
friends, the Freudenburgs, at whose house I several times gave
demonstrations accompanied by lectures. The Freudenburgs were
four or five brothers who shared the direction of the Hermann
Gerson business in Berlin. It was they who first brought me to
Germany, and I was surprised to find them so extremely 'Parisian.'
One of them subscribed to the *Figaro*, and insisted on reading the
whole of it every day, as much in order not to forget his French as to
keep informed of what was happening with us. He astonished me
when he told me that the rôle of Mlle Reichemberg at the Comédie
Française was going to be resumed by Mlle X——; he was much more
in the know than I about all the theatrical gossip. He was a subtle, cultivated man. Lunching with him at Borchardt's, where we ate the
celebrated Hamburg chickens, I asked him some troubling questions
as to the political attitude of Germany, and her military effectives. I
asked him if he did not fear another collision between Germany and
France. He answered me with the customary clichés; the invention of
modern artillery had made any encounter improbable; one could
not think of so monstrous a thing; and besides, Germany was animated by pacific intentions; the Kaiser did not want war; at the price
of certain concessions in Morocco he could be kept quiet for a long
time (it was before Agadir). On the same evening I was invited to the
opera, where Caruso was singing. In the front, on the left, was the
Kaiser with the Empress, and I observed him with an infinite curiosity; but what held my attention above all was another group,
containing all the generals in full dress. They pointed out to me Von
Kluck who had little gold glasses, from behind which there gleamed
a cunning glance. I could imagine him delivering some terrible
stroke against us. He had a lizard's face, his neck was corded, and this
gave the rictus of his mouth a nervous, cruel expression. They also
pointed out to me Von der Goltz, Von Seekt, Hindenburg, and
others.

'But,' said my neighbour, 'it is on Von Kluck that we place our greatest hopes, in case of need.'

And when I said to him, that this was a contradiction of his prognostications in the morning:

'War may come,' he said, 'but not with France.'

Four years later, it came.

It was through this Freudenberg that I was presented to Prince Eitel, one of the three sons of the Kaiser, and the one best versed in the arts. I was surprised to find him so well informed about all our developments, both literary and artistic. Our painting was familiar to him. He knew the names of all our celebrities and 'stars' of the day. He was interested in my models, and knew the names of all the great dress designers of the time, with their specialities. In a word, he was up to the minute, which I found very admirable. For did our Ministers of Fine Arts, for their part, know anything about Max Reinhardt and his creations in the theatre, the performances of *Joan of Arc* he was giving in London, and in which he studied the great crowd-movements which were to light M. Gemier's passionate enthusiasm ten years later? Were they *au courant* with the exhibitions in the Cassirer Gallery? Did they visit the Exhibitions of Cologne and Munich? Were they even informed of them?

In Berlin and Vienna I went to all the exhibitions of the decorative arts. It was then that I made the acquaintance of the chiefs of the Schools, such as Hoffmann, the creator and director of the *Wiener Werkstatte*, Karl Witzmann, M. Muthesius, Wimmer, Bruno Paul, and Klimt.

In passing I must give grateful thanks to Mme Zuckerkandle, who directed my steps in these pioneer artistic circles.

In Berlin I met a whole swarm of architects who were seeking for the New, and sometimes found it. Doubtless they were inspired by the past, and drew their ideas from classic sources. But who would think of reproaching them for that? I spent whole days in visiting modern interiors, built and arranged with such a wealth of new ideas that I had seen nothing like them at home. The villas around Berlin, standing in pine forests, on the borders of lakes, surrounded by gardens full of surprises, seemed to me delicious. I dreamed of creating in France a movement of ideas that should be capable of propagating a new mode in decoration and furnishing.

I was not a blind admirer of all I saw. No, I seriously disapproved certain romantic tendencies, which have always made the creations of Germany heavy, and weighed them down. I remember especially the salon in which I had to give my first lecture, at Hermann Gerson's. I burst out laughing when I saw it, at the risk of stabbing to the heart the artist, or rather the professor, who had conceived this ensemble. I have forgotten his name now, but I shall always see his image, a sort of pinched, emaciated, livid, thin-lipped, gold spectacled Doctor Faustus, with a peruke of white hair thrown back like the mane of a sick and agèd lion. I had never seen an artist who looked like that; his decorations were like himself. He had covered the walls of the salon where I was to receive my audience with bright blue drapery from top to bottom, and from this chapel there flung out sheaves of lilies, as if for the burial of Ophelia. It was so pompous, so solemn, so pretentious that it made me shiver, and I needed a great deal of courage and skill to thaw my listeners.

But for one error of this sort I saw a great many admirable things. It was in Berlin that I saw Shakespeare interpreted in the most living way. *A Midsummer Night's Dream* produced by Reinhardt, *The Taming of the Shrew* and *Much Ado about Nothing*, as well as a 'Shylock,' from which Gemier borrowed most of the discoveries so much lauded by the French press, consoled me for *Penthesilea, Queen of the Amazons.*

Out of curiosity I went specially to Brussels to visit the home of M. Stocklet, built by the architect Hoffmann, of Vienna, who had designed not only the house and its dependencies, but also the garden, the carpets, the furniture, the lighting, the plates, the cutlery, Madame's dresses, and Monsieur's sticks and cravats. This substitution of the taste of the architect for the personality of the proprietors has always seemed to me a sort of slavery – a subjection that makes me smile. I must ask M. and Mme Stocklet to forgive me, for they were unforgettable hosts.

On my return to Paris, after several journeys for study, I established a School of Decorative Art to which I gave the name of one of my girls, *Martine.* I had seen the *herr professors* of Berlin and Vienna torturing the brains of their pupils to make them fit into a new mould like an iron corselet. In Vienna they dissected flowers and bouquets into lozenges and out of them made geometrical figures, whose monotonous repetition did in the long run create a style,

One of the first creations of
Paul Poiret, at Doucet's

Design from Poiret's first major
collection. From the album *Les
Robes de Paul Poiret, racontées par
Paul Iribe*, plate 4, 1908
NAL

Paul Poiret aboard his
houseboat on the Loire canals

Arrival of the houseboat at the
Exposition Des Arts Décoratifs,
Paris, 1925

In Paris, on the terrace of the
Salle Playel, c. 1925

Poiret at work

Lipnitzki/Roger-Viollet/Topfoto

With some of his mannequins at
Victoria Station, London, 1924

Topham Picture Point © 1999/Topfoto

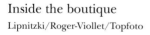

Inside the boutique
Lipnitzki/Roger-Viollet/Topfoto

Evening dress by Poiret, 1928
Lipnitzki/Roger-Viollet/Topfoto

The boutique entrance,
Paris, 1925
Lipnitzki/Roger-Viollet/Topfoto

Poiret assists a model with a
fitting, 1930s

The garden at the end of 'The Thousand-and-Second Night'

Poiret and his family, Paris, 1930
Lipnitzki/Roger-Viollet/Topfoto

An interior decorated by Poiret

really not very different from the Biedermayer. I considered this work and this sort of disciplining of minds absolutely criminal. I wished to provide a counterpoise for all that, and this is how I proceeded:

I scoured the working class districts around Paris for little girls of about twelve, who had just finished their schooling. I set aside several rooms in my house for them, and I put them to work copying nature, without any teacher. Naturally, their parents soon discovered they were wasting their time, and I had to promise them stipends and prizes. I rewarded the best designs. After a very few weeks I obtained marvellous results. These children, being made free to do as they liked, soon forgot the false and empirical precepts they had received at school, and rediscovered all the spontaneity and freshness of their natures.

Whenever it was possible I had them taken into the country or the Zoological Gardens, or into conservatories, where each would do a picture according to her own idea, according to whatever motif pleased her best, and they used to bring back the most charming things. There would be fields of ripe corn, starred with marguerites, poppies, and cornflowers; there were baskets of begonias, masses of hortensias, virgin forests through which sped leaping tigers, all done with an untamed naturalness that I wish I could describe in words. I have kept the collection of their works, and I have pages of touching inspiration, which sometimes approach the prettiest pictures of the douanier Rousseau.

It was with the collaboration of these young artists that I formed the collection of stuffs and tissues that influenced all fashion and the whole of modern decorative art in the great days of the *Maison Martine*, which was established a few months after.

My rôle consisted in stimulating their activity and their taste, without ever influencing them or criticising, so that the source of their inspiration should be kept pure and intact. Truth to tell, they had a much greater ascendency over me than I over them, and my only talent consisted in choosing from all their work that which was most suitable for reproduction. Then it was necessary for me to have that industrial courage which consists in having carried out, sometimes at heavy cost, daring compositions whose value may be misunderstood by the public. I spent a great deal of money on this, and I do not regret it, while perhaps my successors may regret that they have not spent it.

To avoid the necessity of having their designs translated by more or less nonunderstanding workers, and to avoid any loss of sensitiveness in their interpretation, I made them learn the craft of *tapis au point noué*, so that they came to weave with their own hands, straight away without any previous design, carpets whence flowered marvellous blossoms, fresh and living as if they had sprung straight from the earth itself. M. Fenaille, who has won for himself great fame in the art of tapestry, and who has given it profound study, was kind enough to help me with his advice and resources.

Where would the *Martine* school have arrived by now, if it had been able to continue? Favoured by this free teaching, there developed certain quite unique personalities. My pupils did not all do the same leaf, when they applied the accents and characteristics of their designs to the same details. Each produced work impregnated with her own temperament. They worked confidently and without any apprehension, which is why their works seem as if gushing from a spring.

If one asked an adult artist to cover for example a large mural surface by a decoration, he would begin by working out a design on a small scale, and he would enlarge its details progressively to cover the proposed surface. There was nothing like that with these girls. In front of a bare wall, four metres high by four broad, they would first set up their ladders and then trace out their design in its actual size. Thus their motifs took immediate importance and value. This result was obtained because there was no teacher to constrain or analyse. They felt free, and happy in their creating. Was it necessary that the meanness of financiers should have destroyed so moving a work, and that these young artists full of promise should have become novelty saleswomen, or fancy shoemakers?

Many artists were passionately enthusiastic about my experiment, and constantly visited the school. I received Rene Piot, the old master Séruzier, Jean Ajalbert, Keeper of the Tapestry Manufacture at Beauvais, and many others. But he who interested himself more than anyone in the *Martine* school was Raoul Dufy. It is from that time that my pleasant relationship with him dates. We had the same inclinations in decoration. His spontaneous and ardent genius had splashed with flowers the green panels of the doors of my dining room in the Pavillon du Butard. We dreamed of dazzling curtains, and gowns decorated à la Botticelli. Without counting the cost I gave Dufy, who was then making his beginnings in life, the means whereby to realise a few of his dreams. In a few weeks we fixed up a printing workshop in a little place in the Avenue de Clichy, that I had specially hired. We discovered a chemist called Zifferlein, as tiresome as a bushel of fleas, but who knew from top to bottom all about colouring matters, lithographic inks, aniline dyes, fats and acids. So here we were, Dufy and I, like Bouvard and Pecuchet, at the head of a new craft, from which we were about to draw new joys and exaltations. But I have not yet described Dufy, who hides his genius beneath the appearance of a grocer's assistant. A rosy-cheeked, blonde archangel, with curly hair, rather dollish, with *petites* gestures, one had to see him in his workshop, walking with short steps, in shirt sleeves, every moment bringing out from his portfolios masterpieces, the least of which is, to-day, worth tens of thousands of francs. Dufy has never ceased to be a simple artist, whose heart and soul are entirely devoted to his work.

His discoveries in art are known, and his substitution of his own conventional expressions for reality. He has artificial procedures to represent water, the earth, harvests, clouds, which to-day, in the world of art-lovers, have achieved as much actuality as the very elements they represent. It was fit work for a genius to substitute for the public's his own vision, and to make it prevail against established notions. When one sees in the street a lamp of a certain shape one knows it signifies that here is a Tube Station: and similarly, when one sees certain of Dufy's arabesques, one knows that they signify water, or foliage; and to-day he has imposed this alphabet, of which he is the author, on the *cognoscenti* of the whole world. How should I not be proud to think that such an artist had his beginnings in the shadow of my own?

Dufy drew for me and cut on wood designs taken from his Bestiary. From them he created sumptuous stuffs, out of which I made dresses which have, I hope, never been destroyed. Somewhere there must be *amateurs* who preserve these relics.

After we had spent a great deal of money and much time in getting together our first *materiel* (our first boiler was a wooden one), and in carrying out our first trials, we saw one day the immense, looming silhouette of M. Bianchini, one of the proprietors of the great firm of Atuyer, Bianchini and Férrier, who came to propose to

Dufy that he should provide him with more worthy industrial facilities. Dufy was gentleman enough not to accept without informing me of the proposition which had been made to him, and I was enough of a grandee not to prevent him from furthering his career, although I was to suffer from his defection. For is it necessary to add that no compensation was offered me by M. Bianchini?

I liquidated the little factory in the Avenue du Clichy, and since, I have had the consolation of admiring, in the productions of the Maison Bianchini, all that was due to the collaboration of my friend. There were brocades and prints of utter beauty that one day will rank in the history of decorative art as high as the designs of Philippe de la Salle, or Oberkampf.

To-day Dufy no longer works for M. Bianchini, he has returned to painting, in order that we may have nothing to regret. Decorative art loses a good servant in Dufy, but he could never accept constraint. A man of his genius cannot bend himself to the exigencies of commerce, for commerce wishes to keep only what can be turned to profit. Thus gardeners only retain on a tree those branches which bear fruit, but an artist needs to let all his branches grow, and even those that will produce nothing are valuable to him. Who would dare to say that they too may not produce some result in a more distant future? For an artist the useless is more precious than the necessary, and he is made to suffer when people try to make him admit the inanity of his daring, or when only that which is saleable is chosen from his work. An artist has antennæ that vibrate far ahead of ours, and he has presentiments of the future trends of taste long before the vulgar. The public can never say that he is mistaken; it can only express humility, in matters it cannot understand.

I exhibited, in 1924, fourteen of Dufy's canvases in the pinnace *Orgues*. They were great screens he had executed in Bianchini's factories at Tournon, for the special purpose of decorating my boat. They represented the regattas of Havre, the races at Longchamp, a landscape of the Ile de France, baccarat at Deauville, a ball at the *Prefecture Maritime*, etc. . . . Who remembers them? Nobody noticed them. The public taste was not ripe, yet to-day I could sell them for their weight in gold, so true is it that for works of art and for all genial ideas there is an hour for which one must know how to wait.

This exhibition of decorative arts was, in any case, a great disillusionment for me (I don't mean because of the money I lost over it, for that is in the order of remediable mishaps), for it could not render any service to decorative art. It opened its doors at the time when the Parisians, who constitute the interested clientèle, were departing for the country. Perhaps they could have been kept if fêtes and galas and artistic celebrations worthy of them had been provided, but nothing was done in that direction. The miserable regattas that were given on the Seine only brought together a few poor assemblies. They could neither attract nor hold anybody. At the most, in the evening between 9 and 11, one saw a flood tide of concierges and workpeople who liked lights, a crowd, and noise. I was mistaken to count on a *de luxe* clientèle, for they flee from popular pleasures; they did not come; it is an experience which I shall remember.

The Commissary-General, M. Fernand David, and M. Paul Léon, Director of the Beaux-Arts, had the kindness to tell me that I was unconsciously the instigator and reason for this exhibition for, if I had not created, in 1912, the *Maison Martine*, which had unloosed so many imitators and a flourishing movement of decorative ideas, this exhibition could never have taken place. Modest though I be, I think they were right. But the exhibition when it did take place ought to have been made a success. The reason for its failure is to be seen in the fact that it was directed and organised by the old, while by definition it was the work of youth. But all youthfulness was snuffed out. This, moreover, speaking more generally, is what causes our present troubles in France. This stifling of youth, in a people that ought always to remain the most youthful in the world, is a fact about which radical explanations must be given one day very soon. The country is to such a point given up to gerontocracy that the young no longer dare, and no longer even think, of claiming the place due to them in politics, after the war that was by them waged. Yet they should have some right to build for themselves the foundations for what remains to them of the future.

I had a conversation on this subject, one day at a friend's, with a deputy who is to-day a Minister of the Republic, and who that evening was parading a hearty contempt of public opinion. I allowed myself this simple phrase: 'If the public heard you!'

Then rising like a Tribune of the Revolution, this pocket Mirabeau cried out: 'The Public? Slaves, slaves!' I will not name him, for charity's sake, but he will recognise himself.

XI
At Work

The business journeys I undertook in every direction did not prevent me from also travelling for the sake of study, whereby I furnished my mind with memories and precious treasures. The principal work of a creator, during the hours when he does not create, is precisely to embellish his brain as one embellishes one's house, and to accumulate artistic riches from museums and from all the beauties of nature. The more subtlety and refinement he has acquired, the more his work will reflect it, for a sort of assimilation and digestion takes place, whereby his hands give forth the beauty that is within him. If this is not true, from a scientific point of view, I have always acted as if I believed it, and I do believe it.

Naturally, these innumerable travels, plus the worry of business and a constant search for the new, implied a good deal of fatigue. I had iron health, that allowed me to go to bed at any time of night, and be at my work at nine in the morning without losing one iota of my good humour. Every morning I did an hour's fencing or gymnastics with friends, who came to my garden. Boussingault, Segonzac and Ditte, now a notary. After two or three assaults with the *épée*, we had a cold shower, and a glass of port crowned the exercise; and at a quarter to nine I was at my desk, with a clear and ready mind. I prepared the day's programme with great order and method, but I always accepted with pleasure any fortuitous circumstance that obliged me to change it.

One day when I was closeted in my office seeking out new forms with a *première* and some mannequins, a telephone call summoned me to go to M. Henri Bataille's; I was to go at once with Ronsin, to hear him read his next play, whose *mise-en-scène* he wanted to confide to us. Ronsin came to fetch me, we leapt into the Hispano-Suiza, and so to Villers-Cotterets.

Henri Bataille lived in an old château he had had restored, at Vivières. The portrait of the author of *Phalène* has doubtless often been described, so I will only say that on me he has always produced the effect of a sun-tanned Pierrot, of a basic sadness, and surrounded by an atmosphere of boredom that is exceedingly distinguished, but exceedingly artificial. It was of him that Cocteau whispered to me one day, during a rehearsal, 'He thinks his enteritis is a vice!' On that day we found him in a most affected pose, lying rather than sitting in an immense leather armchair, wedged in pillows. He thought he had a broken arm, from which he suffered, so he said, a great deal, and he actually did have his left arm in a sling. Wherefore he would profit by this forced immobility to read us bits from his last play, which was *L'homme à la Rose*. While he was talking to us in the great green salon on the ground floor of the château, we saw Yvonne de Bray enter, accompanied by three greyhounds, and carrying a bunch of roses in her very pretty arms. The greyhounds, the bunch of roses, the muslin dress, the great shepherdess straw hat, this sudden ray of sunshine in the depths of the scene – where had I seen it all? It was certainly a theatrical entry, and it was all artificial. I was the dupe of a dream, or rather, I was not! It was the exact cover of the fashion journal *Vogue*. Bataille, enchanted by this apparition, tried to spy in Ronsin's and my eyes the effect produced on us. He must have been disillusioned. As the lovely artiste approached him to kiss his forehead, he withdrew his wounded arm from its sling, and cautiously bending it, drew to himself her who was the object of his passion; then, carelessly, and thinking of something else, he forgot which arm it was, and put back the other into the sling. Ronsin and I exchanged a look of suppressed laughter. There was a diversion and we passed into the dining-room. A cordial luncheon . . . and a frugal one. In a brace of shakes we were having our coffee on the terrace. Mlle de Bray presented us to her llama, for she had a llama, a strange black giraffe, with a horse's body, which could not bear the sight of Mme de Bray, her mother, and continually spat at her.

Soon after we went back to work in Bataille's study. He really made us tremble with excitement as he read us extracts from his work, and communicated to us his creative flame, in such sort that on the way back, we thought of nothing but how to realise his intentions, and give his dream concrete form. There were in his piece singular beauties and opportunities to use with effect unique settings, for instance the scene in which Don Juan looks on at his own burial in the cathedral, for which we took inspiration from the great gates of the cathedral of Seville. I still see the grey of the walls, with the mourning black and the liturgical red. And what ravishing artists were Mary Marquet and Mona Delza, in her robe of cloth of silver encrusted with silver lace, with a vermilion comb veiled in the silver mantilla thrown over her dark hair. It was impossible to say where fiction began and exact reconstitution ended, for I had married history and my own fantasy, and after soaking myself in the spirit of the modes of the time of Don Juan, I had interpreted them with the greatest freedom.

What nights we spent in the theatre, in order to get a faultless ensemble! Dawn would find us still at work. Léon Volterra knew how to improvise suppers that revived the ardour of his collaborators. I would get home at five in the morning, utterly exhausted; I would sleep three hours, and at eight o'clock I was fencing under the direction of good Maître Cherbuquet who, for his part, could not understand that one could be tired. At nine o'clock I was duly at work, and I drove and directed my whole concern till noon, then, in order to avoid sleeping after lunch, for one must always be elegant, I would go to the country by car – I would perhaps hear, in some little inn at Bonnières, an accordion that would bring tears to my eyes; I would pack the player into my car, and bring him back to Paris, where I was having to dinner Rip, that so Parisian author of the only amusing revues. The accordion made my guests dance the whole evening, and at two in the morning I had the neighbouring gallery opened in order to show them an exhibition of Greco or Manet. Next morning I was at the Sorbonne where I was seeking, with Professor Charles Henri, the mastery of a process of phosphorescent tinting, with which I produced a new effect at the music hall a few weeks later. Together we sought to materialise luminous colours. Charles Henri was not only a learned chemist, he was a distinguished gourmet, and he understood wines – he even gave copious advice to a certain great Vouvray grower, with whom he used to spend his holidays. We lunched together at the end of our morning's work, and he had his own personal views about the physiology of taste. Then I returned to my house, where Countess Greffulhe was trying on a golden dress she was to wear at the Madeleine on her daughter's wedding day.

In the salon where she stood moulded by this marvellous sheath of metal, bordered with sable, there reigned an awe as if in a fairy's chamber. The saleswoman inclined her head, ravished, the *première* passed an artist's hand over the seams of the stuff, and through the bullseye window of the door one could see the eager, indiscreet faces of the staff, and could hear their flattering exclamations: 'What a miracle!' Or else: 'There is splendour for you!' The Countess, haughty and morose amidst this concert of praise, lifted her head and pointed her nose in every direction. When I came in, I bowed to her and said she had reason to be satisfied, for her dress was very beautiful. Then, lifting her head, so that her ill humour should fall from as high as possible, she said to me:

'I thought that you only knew how to dress midinettes and hussies, but I did not know that you were capable of making a dress for a great lady.'

I answered her, that her robe had in precise fact been made by these midinettes, and that the great ladies of Belgium could always trust themselves to the taste of the midinettes of Paris, and they would only gain thereby. And I left the place absolutely scandalised to find, in a woman of her age and her opulence, such lack of tact, joined with such perfidy and conceit. My words were repeated by my staff. In Russia they would have deserved the knout, in Italy, castor oil, in France, they made everyone laugh. When she came to me again, to order more dresses, her revengeful saleswoman named such enormous prices that she was not rich enough to pay them.

I have only recounted all this, and the way I employed my time during several days, in order to let you see the charming diversity of my occupations, which yet had one single end, that of making women more seductive. The life of a dress designer unrolls like a cinema film, varied but continuous. Add to what I have described my visits to the workrooms necessitated by the *Maison Martine*, where there was being made simultaneously the furnishings for a private house for Mlle Spinelly (I am afraid it was never paid for) and a dining-room for my old master Doucet, for his apartment in the Bois de Boulogne. For M. Jacques Doucet, forgetting his former legitimate disillusionments, had found me worthy to execute one of the settings of his private life. I gave myself to this task passionately, summoning to my aid the great artist Fauconnet, who designed the detail of the panels. I have not yet said anything about Fauconnet, who was the most wise and devoted of my collaborators in the *Maison Martine*. He was an

artist of indescribable charm, with a mind as penetrating as it was profound, a sort of philosopher of the olden time, full of a rare irony and
scepticism. He designed with a line as fine and as subtle as his
thought, and his processes of expression had the same acuity as his
processes of observation. He was truly erudite in artistic matters, and
everything he did in line as in colour was influenced by his classic culture. It was he who designed the programme of the fête that I gave in
the Pavillon du Butard, inspired by the Corinthian vases whereon a
black ivy runs over the tender colour of the clay. He designed all the
inscriptions that decorated Mlle Spinelly's hall. He was torn from his
friends by a premature death, and his career did not have the fullness
it deserved, but there is a fine canvas by him in the Luxembourg, and
pages that assure his fame. I have seen Fauconnet piercing for days
on end little pale yellow shells he gathered on the sands of the isle of
Tudy, in Brittany, where we spent our holidays. He made charming
necklets out of them, which he wore himself, and made his friends
wear too. With us there were Naudin, his wife, and his sons.

We had come to the isle of Tudy to a house I had hired by
letter. When I arrived I was very taken aback to find it bare and
ill-furnished; the dining-room was completely whitewashed, like a
Trappist's cell. Perhaps that might please me to-day; it did not please
me then. The place was solitary and desolate, but Naudin's talent
made a crowd of people appear, and the walls of the dining-room
were covered with inscriptions. On a red and white awning, one read
'Café du Commerce,' and customers of every social rank, sailors and
rich shipowners, were represented seated before *apéritifs*.

It was an agreeable company, and we spent jolly moments with
these gentry, imagining their reflections and observations. The buffet
and the chairs cut a sad figure in the richness of this setting; we
painted them green, and the whole developed a wild gaiety – but
what was less gay was the owner, on the day of our departure. He went
scarlet with anger. This narrow Breton, who might have turned to his
profit a dining-room decorated by Naudin, did not understand his
good fortune. He summoned me in the local court, and I was
ordered to restore everything to its original condition.

Then I visited London again, to put the final touch to the costumes
I had made for *Afgar*, a spectacular operetta which was played for

three years continuously under the management of Charles Cochran at the Pavilion Theatre. What Englishman has not seen *Afgar*, nor heard the beautiful Delysia, who became a London 'star' under the ægis of this skilled manufacturer of 'stars.'

Delysia, who had been but a singer in Paris, became a *cantatrice* in London, where she was fêted, adulated, and triumphantly received. In London she received Marshal Foch, and I still remember the day I passed with her in the company of the greatest glories of the music hall of the day, Little Tich, George Robey, and the droll Morton.

I visited the South Kensington Museum, which is full of the treasures of the Indies. There I found the most precious documents relative to Indian art and manners. In particular there was a collection of turbans that enchanted me. Every kind of way of putting on these headdresses and fixing them on the head was represented. I admired unwearyingly the diversity of their so logical and so elegant forms. There was the little close turban of the sepoys, that ends in a panel negligently thrown over the shoulder; and there was the enormous Rajah's turban, mounted like a gigantic pin-cushion, to receive all the costliest aigrettes and jewels. I at once obtained from the keeper permission to work from these magnificent specimens. I was even allowed to take the turbans from their cases and caress them. I immediately telegraphed to Paris for one of my *premières*. I inspired her with my own flame, and she spent eight days in the Museum, imitating and copying, reproducing the models she had before her eyes: a few weeks later, we had made turbans the fashion in Paris.

It was the period of the first Russian Ballets. M. Diaghileff had launched on the world his pleiad of 'stars' who for a good many years were to illuminate several fields of art. The Baksts, the Nijinskys, the Karsavinas, shone with all their brilliance. Like many French artists, I was very struck by the Russian Ballet, and I should not be surprised if it had a certain influence on me. But it must be clearly stated that I already existed, and that my reputation was made, long before that of M. Bakst. Only foreign journalists could make any mistake about that and, voluntarily or involuntarily, commit the error of making my work the descendant of Bakst's. Nothing is commoner than this misunderstanding amongst the profane and the ill-informed; I have always combated it, for despite all the admiration I had for Bakst, I always refused to work after his designs. I know too well what happens in such cases. When the costume succeeds, the designer takes the credit of having created it, and if it fails, he alleges he was betrayed by the dressmaker's interpretation. I wanted to avoid such misunderstanding, in his interest as in my own, for I was persuaded that it is one thing to make a water-colour, where one has the right of faking proportions and attitudes, and where one can give a conventional expression, but quite another to make a rainbow costume, for instance, for a woman who presents herself with her form already determined, and often incompatible with the character she wants to give herself.

I displeased more than one of my clients who came to me with some pretty water-colour bought very expensively from Bakst, because I refused to interpret the intentions of another. This attitude was taken for jealousy on my part. It was nothing of the sort; besides I could not accept without discrimination all Bakst's ideas, for too often he had recourse to exaggeration and excess to achieve a style. And there was little to be got from his theatrical creations. They were much too exaggerated to inspire a dressmaker, who works in the realism of life; and if Bakst did exercise any influence over me, it can only have been a very indirect one.

In a general way, I believe I borrowed very few elements from the artists of my time. The dominant tendency, that of Cubism, which for thirty years has exercised a crushing dictatorial dominion, did not allow me to apply its principles in my field. I was not unaware of Picasso's researches, but I have always considered them as studio exercises and mental speculations, which should not have gone beyond a circle of artists, and about which the public ought to have known nothing. The danger has been that the public has taken these analytic elucubrations for completed works, whereas they were only studies and explanatory decompositions. The evolution of Picasso's art seems to be proving me right to-day, since after passing his youth in analytical works, he seems to have returned to a more accessible synthesis. I am unable to consider without a certain antipathy the rôle played by this artist, who, personally, I like very much, but who in history will have the sad responsibility of having led astray so many sheep, and having inebriated so many excellent enthusiasms. How many artists sincerely in love with a more human ideal has he lost to us, in return for two or three talents he has perhaps revealed to us within the narrow limits of Cubism.

XII
The Fêtes I Gave

I wanted to find means for keeping my friends near me, and creating a centre that should be the capital of all Parisian taste and intelligence. I succeeded: when I gave a party, no one failed to answer my summons, no previous engagement could avail against my invitation.

I could not now remember all the fêtes I gave, but I want to speak of the *Fête des Rois*, which will make the post-war generation realise how we amused ourselves aforetime.

I had sent out invitations in which King Louis XIV himself (the rôle of the King was entrusted to Decroix) invited my friends to be present at his *Petit Lever*; and to each he allotted a rôle and a personality. Thus he said to Bagnolet: 'You are Biron, the King's coiffeur'; to Segonzac: 'You are Champagne, His Majesty's first valet'; to Marcelle Collet: 'You are Mlle de la Vallière'; to Bastien de Beaupré, who believed it from the moment he received the invitation: 'You are Turenne!' – he espoused his rôle to such an extent, and so intensely studied his personality, that he arrived at the fête bearing in his cuirass the bullet that had killed him. Falling down in the middle of the proceedings, and having seriously hurt his skull on the marble lintel of the door as he was dancing the minuet with Mme de Maintenon, he refused to admit that he was losing blood by his wound, and to friends who pressed him to get himself attended to, he replied:

'I have seen blood flow . . .'

On that evening all my guests, as they arrived, were led to the King's bedside; the tapestry curtains of the baldaquin were closed, and the royal chamber was in a peaceful twilight. Little by little the courtiers grouped themselves respectfully twenty paces from the bed whereon reposed His Majesty, whose snoring could be heard through the Gobelins. Then the doctors and apothecaries entered, and enquired of the First Valet de Chambre how His Majesty had slept, and Dunoyer de Segonzac gave them the most intimate and reassuring details. Then the night-stool was brought, and the King, with a great yawn, desired the kiss of Mlle de la Vallière, who advanced uneasily beneath the eye of Maintenon and Montespan. Then the King rose and at once received his coiffeur who, as he adjusted his peruke, gave him a tip for the races: 'Back Roy-Soleil, to win.'

The King's tailor handed him his Sunday tunic, and the King came down to the dining-room, where a grandiose breakfast and a spectacle right worthy of Versailles awaited him.

You ought to have seen Louis XIV come down the steps of the stair of honour, followed at a distance by his courtiers and marquesses but preceded by the valets who walked backwards to light the King with their candelabra, to have any idea of the conscientiousness and pains Decroix had devoted to his rôle, despite rather amateur resources. His stick, in particular, was made of a billiard cue, artistically camouflaged, and until five in the morning we could not approach our comrade without calling him Majesty, and showing him the utmost respect. He wanted to be King, and he was.

It was on returning from a Bal des Quat' Z'Arts, in the month of May 1911, I think, that I decided to give, in my salons and gardens in Paris, an unforgettable fête, that I called 'The Thousand-and-Second Night.' I had gathered together several artists, and I put my resources at their disposal to realise an ensemble that no one had been able to create before. The artists all strove to answer my appeal to their utmost, and that is what created the marvel I am about to describe.

My house was closed by tapestries, in such sort that glances from the street could not penetrate. The guests were received as in a theatre by a squad of old gentlemen in evening dress, who were no jokers, and most carefully scanned the arrivals.

'Excuse me, sir, you are in evening dress. This is a costume fête, and you cannot come in.'

'But, sir, my dress clothes are covered by an authentic Chinese mantle.'

'Monsieur, we are not in China, we are in Persia, and your costume has nothing to do with the setting. Therefore I cannot let you enter unless you change your costume.'

'At this time of night, it is impossible.'

'Excuse me, sir, if you will be good enough to go up to the first floor, a Persian costume can be provided for you, according to authentic documents; it will do you honour, and will not disfigure the ensemble of the fête.'

(I knew the carelessness of some of my friends, and I had taken measures to counteract it.)

A few refused to dress to my taste, and retired; others, better advised, accepted the dress I imposed on them.

The guests, thus combed out, passed in little groups into a second salon where a half-naked negro, draped in Bokhara silk, armed with a torch and a yataghan, marshalled them and led them to me. First they crossed a sanded court where, beneath a blue and gold tent, fountains gushed in porcelain basins. One would have thought it the sun-filled patio of Aladdin's palace. Through the colours of the tent there fell a multi-coloured light.

They went up several steps and found themselves in front of an immense golden cage, barred with twisted iron grilles, inside which I had shut up my favourite (Mme Poiret) surrounded by her ladies of honour, who sang real Persian airs. Mirrors, sherbert, aquariums, little birds, chiffons and plumes, such were the distractions of the Queen of the Harem and her ladies of honour. Then one penetrated into a salon where there was a jet of water that seemed to gush out from the tapestry, and fell back into a basin of iridescent crystal.

In the next room, whither one proceeded through wide doors, piled-up cushions, multi-coloured, plain or richly embroidered, made a hill at whose summit was seated the great tragedian De Max. He was dressed in a black silk *gandura*, and wore round his neck innumerable pearls, saltier-wise. He told me that one of his friends, an American lady, had entrusted him that evening with all her jewels (there were three million francs' worth). He told stories taken from the *Thousand and One Nights*, one finger raised in the air according to the gesture of Oriental storytellers, and a crowd of male and female idlers were all agape in a circle round him.

Without stopping here, one went on to the garden, which was dark and mysterious. Carpets covered the flags of the steps and the sand of the alleys, so that the noise of steps was deadened and there reigned a great silence. The fascinated explorers spoke in a low voice, as in a mosque. In the middle of embroidered *parterres* was the vase of white cornelian announced in the programme. Masked lights hidden in the surrounding foliage lit it up strangely. From the vase escaped a narrow stream of water, like those one sees in Persian engravings, and pink ibises walked all about to take their part in the freshness and light. Certain trees were covered with dark blue luminous fruit; others had bays of violet light. Monkeys, parrots, and parrakeets, all alive, animated all this verdure, which seemed as if the entrance to a great park. I could be seen in the depths of it, like some swarthy white-bearded Sultan, holding an ivory whip. Around me, on the steps of my throne, all my lascivious concubines lay at full length, appearing to await and fear my anger. Hither the guests were conducted in small groups, to make their obeisance according to the tradition of Islam.

When my three hundred guests were all present, I rose and, followed by all my women, went toward the cage of my favourite, to whom I restored her freedom. She flew out like a bird, and I precipitated myself in pursuit of her, cracking my useless whip. She was lost in the crowd. Did we know, on that evening, that we were rehearsing the drama of our lives?

Then the buffets opened, and the spectacles began. Hidden orchestras played softly, as if to respect the calm splendour of this intoxicating night. And all night long I took pleasure in playing on the sensibility of my guests as on a clavier. Two of my friends continually came to me to receive my instructions, and I gave them the signal for the successive attractions, which were planned to be of increasing interest.

In one corner was the booth of the pythoness, who had encrusted diamonds in her teeth. There was the potter who cast little clay vessels with stiff but cunning fingers. And then suddenly there appeared the monkey merchant, covered all over by animals that climbed over his shoulders and head, their eyes glinting maliciously as they uttered strident cries. And here was the dusky bar, where only the liqueurs were luminous. What alchemist had prepared the startling phantasmagoria of this disturbing laboratory? . . . A hundred long-necked carafes, a hundred crystal ewers contained all the beverages whose gamut extends from violet anisette and garnet bitters to emerald crême-de-menthe and golden citronella, by way of milky Advokaats and the acidulated crimson of grenadine. Then there was liquorice, and almond emulsion, Chartreuse, gins, vermouths, orangeades, kirsches, and prunella. All the painters who were my guests entered in and played as with a palette with these pure tints, which they mixed as they pleased in the transparency of their long glasses. Thus they created mysterious and sinful drinks that were a feast to see and a surprise to taste.

Then Regina Badet danced on the lawn, whose grass was not crushed by her feet, so light was she and immaterial. The sight presented by the spectators, seated or lying on cushions and carpets, was not less beautiful than the dance itself; it was a confused mass of silks, jewels, and aigrettes that sparkled iridescently, like stained glass in moonlight.

And after that Trouhanova danced, a fantastic and generous houri. Then the exquisite, delicate Zambelli, fleeing the ardours of an agile, passionate mime. Later, fronded leaves came up, and from the level of the ground flames and sparks in sheaves which rose noiseless as high as the leaves, and then spread out like glass flowers.

Then a cataract of fire crowned the palace, and suddenly the air resounded with a rending thunder. From the terrace that dominated the garden there rushed a luminous rain that fell to earth on the steps of the perron. Everyone feared the tapestries might be set alight. By turns silver and gold, this exciting storm electrified the assembly, and when it ceased, it left behind phosphorescent insects hanging to the branches and suspended everywhere in mid-air. The monkeys and parrakeets, disturbed in their sleep, uttered terrified cries. Dawn found them distracted, breaking the chains that kept them in the branches, the birds taking wing, the monkeys fleeing with great leaps over the neighbouring roofs, toward the Champs Elysées.

While twenty negroes and twenty negresses plied censers with myrrh and incense, whose blue flames made the air fragrant with balm, a flute and a zither were heard in the thicket, stirring the senses. Hindoo cooks prepared hors d'œuvres and culinary specialities after their fashion, using the fruits and produce and artifices of their land.

In the morning, the painter Fauconnet was to be seen amusing and astonishing the assembly with an orange, which he made disappear and reappear like a fakir, dressed in a white robe like that of a professional juggler or magician.

The gathering was composed of artists and sensitive amateurs, who set themselves in unison and sought to increase by their presence the interest and effect of this grandiose festivity. The wealthiest of them, like Princess Murat and M. Boni de Castellane, have often repeated that they had never in their lives seen anything as thrilling as the spectacles that filled this miraculous night.

Naturally there have been people who have said that I gave these fêtes as an item of advertisement, but I want to destroy this insinuation, which can only have originated in stupidity.

I have never believed in the virtue of advertisement, and if I have had a great deal given me, it is because it has been offered to me gratuitously, for I am not among those who pay in order to be spoken of.

These fêtes, in which I gathered together all my friends, did me a great deal of harm among my enemies, and raised against me those who had not had the good fortune to be admitted to them. One knows what happens in Paris – they revenged themselves ignobly by telling scandalous stories, as false as contemptible.

A short time after this a lady of the aristocracy asked me to go to see her. She wanted to consult me about a fête she desired to give to her friends, to be called 'The Thousand-and-Second Night.' I stopped her immediately, to give her its real number: One Thousand and Three, and I pointed out to her that the Thousand-and-Second had been given a few days before, by me. She asked me to give her some advice as to how to make the best of her house. I saw a fairly large gallery, and I counselled her to make it into an alley of cypresses like those in Persian miniatures. Naturally it would be necessary to take away the pictures that were on the walls, and keep them somewhere else for a few days.

'Oh,' she cried, 'my husband would never agree to taking down these marvels, he is most attached to them.'

'At any rate you will surely remove these Louis XV settees, which have nothing Oriental about them, and these shepherdesses, which are not in the character of the fête.'

'Not for anything in the world,' cried the fair lady. 'They are family pieces, and they are the honour of my house. They cannot be moved without risk.'

Upon this I ceased to interest myself in Mme de Ch——'s projects. Her fête took place: it was charming and brilliant.

Boni de Castellane approved me, Boni de Castellane who was a great connoisseur in all matters of festivities; wherefore I am sensible of the opinion he formed about the parties he participated in chez moi. The fêtes that were once given at the Duchesse de Doudeauville's, he told me, were sometimes fatuous enough, but certainly did not pour out those treasures of imagination and decorative invention that I spent without measure.

Boni de Castellane and M. Robert de Rothschild who, by their station in the world, were in a position to appreciate everything that was done in Paris in this kind, awarded me the palm. But I invited few men of the world, for I was pleased to associate with the artists who were MY world only those *amateurs* worthy to understand and love them.

Boni de Castellane, whose silhouette is known to all the world, would have been the Master of the Ceremonies under another régime. He loved the old and accepted the new, and he was above all, a man of discernment and distinction. He chose in the way one opens the pages of a book with a paper knife – not at all at hazard, but with an implacable certainty and precision. His taste was incapable of betraying him. It was at the performance of *Minaret* that I saw him for the first time, elegant in his black suit, his head high and haughty, his cane dangling, a provocative and insolent dandy, with a perpetual shrugging of his shoulders and his elbows pressed into his waist. He represented to me the personality I had wanted to create when, once upon a time, I had dreamed of establishing a newspaper.

I had imagined the evocation before all Paris of the figure of a personage whom I called 'The Prince': that was to be the title of the paper. This impertinent and fidgety individual could not keep in one place. He went to first nights, visited exhibitions, went into the shops, had himself shown everything and never thought himself obliged to buy anything, but took away samples of all that pleased him. He had an opinion on every subject under the sun, politics, music, architecture, matters of justice equally with matters of the kitchen, and he never denied himself the pleasure of saying or writing it. And that was exactly what constituted his, or, if you like, my paper. I had dreamed of entrusting cookery to Tristan Bernard, sport to Anatole France, art to Laurent Tailhade, politics to Sacha Guitry, and of making them the four unique collaborators inspiring *The Prince*.

The first visit I made was to Sacha Guitry. The project seemed to please him: he questioned me about the make-up of the paper, or rather, explained to me how he saw it himself, and wanted to make me admire one of those reproductions of masterpieces that the English and Swiss produce by the three-colour process. We could not come to any agreement about the choice of a process so remote from my artistic intentions. I left Guitry very disillusioned, and I never saw him again. I renounced this project but I have never since seen Boni de Castellane without regretting my Prince, of whom he was the perfect incarnation.

Later I organised a great ball at the 'Opera,' at the request of Princess J. Murat. It was a difficult problem to make the 'Opera,' a vast crimson and gold vessel, of a solemnity and luxury long out of fashion, gay; nevertheless I agreed, and I produced the Parrakeet Ball, which I carried out in a harmony of red and violet, insisting on these two colours for the costumes as is the practice in the Provençal carnivals.

I also produced at Cannes, for Cornuché, a series of fêtes which will never be forgotten by those who came to them. I had to find each week a new means of attracting a clientèle that was solicited throughout the whole coast by varied attractions. There was a Golden Fête, a Paris Fête, a New York Fête, etc. . . . and each served as a pretext for a distribution of appropriate favours, that were positively fought for, in spite of the good manners that reigned everywhere. I ceased to interest myself in these celebrations on the day Jean-Gabriel Domergue wanted to undertake them.

Chapter XIII
The Pavillon du Butard

One day as I was walking in the woods of Fausses-Reposes with my friend Desclers, by chance in my wanderings I happened upon a stone pavilion that was an architectural marvel. I found out that it had been built by Ange-Marie Gabriel, the architect of the Trianon and of the two great palaces in the Place de la Concorde. Louis XV had need of a rendezvous near Versailles where he could unbutton after hunting, and he had ordered this folly to be constructed for him. He had used it occasionally. Louis XVI also had come, notably on the day when his Swiss Guards were murdered, and the debonair, indifferent King wrote on that same day in his diary: 'Been to the Butard, killed a swallow.' A happy nature!

Other sovereigns had been there, and Napoleon I himself, who made use of all the luxuries of his predecessors. Then, under the ægis of the Republic, everything had fallen into abandonment and ruin, despite the zeal of keepers insufficiently provided with resources. I therefore thought of approaching the competent authorities, and asking them to give me the right to repair the cornices, restore the fallen vaults, and maintain this marvellous bit of art at my own cost, in return for which I should be authorised to inhabit it.

A few weeks after, the pavilion was let to me, at an exceedingly modest rent, but I spent a great deal on it. I had to have water brought, and a lavatory, and other conveniences which the King of France had done without. And I wanted to restore to this gem its former lustre and majesty. I spent an enormous sum to acquire an Aubusson carpet and a suite of chairs and couches that were exactly right to furnish it. Candelabra of the period, genuine affairs in which the candles of the period were burnt, a harpsichord, and antique musical instruments; a viola da gamba, a viola d'amore, pocket violins, hung all along the wooden panels. The musicians of the seventeenth and eighteenth centuries, Gluck, Rameau, Daquin, and Couperin, were played, and the pavilion resumed the smiles of its happiest days.

The *Parent* Quartette gave a concert of ancient music there one day, for which my friend Naudin had designed the programme, with a picture representing the musicians of the old days gathered round a harpsichord beneath the cupola of the great salon to play a minuet by Couperin. A personage standing on the right was Naudin's own portrait.

The success of this delicate fête made me think of reconstructing for my friends one of the Kermesses of Versailles. I gathered together my artist comrades, and I let them into the secret of my design. Naudin found a ballet by Lulli called *Les Festes de Bacchus*, which could be reconstructed with the aid of taste and ingenuity. We possessed both. Rameau's cantatas, *Diana and Acteon* and *Impatience* were also exhumed, and finally we reconstructed a ballet of the sixteenth century by G. Gastoldi, with music by Pallacivino, wherein there successively appeared the following personages: The Man in a Hurry, The Dancing Master, The Courtesan, The Bully, The Prisoner, The Lovesick Swain, The Serenader, The Tormented One, and The Candle Snuffer. The scene took place on a boarded stage, as in the time of Tabarin.

The fête took place on the 20th June, 1912. The argument was as follows: I had supposed that all the gods and goddesses, nymphs, naiads, dryads and satyrs in the Park of Versailles had secretly given one another rendezvous in the neighbouring wood, at the Pavillon du Butard – so all my guests had to borrow the features of some personage belonging to the mythology of Louis XIV. They nearly all arrived in their cars, which were parked in a corner of the forest, but a few 'buses started from the Place de la Concorde, and brought from Paris those inhabitants of Olympus who did not possess automobiles. They were driven through the city at speed, in order to give no hint to the curious. On their arrival, they were greeted by nymphs veiled in white, bearing torches, who escorted them through the dark, through the great trees of the forest, toward the Pavilion where, with solemnity, I received them, dressed as the Chryselephantine statue of Olympian Jove, with curled golden hair, curled golden beard, draped in an ivory veil, and shod with buskins. All that part of the forest that had been let to me, and in which the fête was to take place, had been decorated in the spirit of the great century. In one place there was a grandiose buffet, beneath tunnelled trellises, and twenty maîtres d'hôtel all in white proceeded to distribute the crowns and garlands and the festoons of fruit that garnished the tables. Pyramids of water-melons, pomegranates, and pineapples deployed a rich decorative architecture. In another place there was a rural eating house, a sort of cookshop for the soldiers of the King, in which Bacchic serving-women crowned with vine leaves poured out new wine. Behind them piled-up barrels promised gaiety enough. In front were tubs filled with scarlet shrimps, baskets full of grapes, cherries and gooseberries. A Bacchante distributed horns like those from which the shepherds of Arcady were wont to drink. One had to take a horn, fill it from the barrel and empty it at a gulp . . . but the point of the horn is long, and contains much wine.

I had three hundred guests. During the night they drank eight hundred quarts of champagne, and the scene was so beautiful and the spirit of the fête so elevated that no scandal, no unpleasantness occurred, and everything proceeded in perfect order. The appearance of each artist was the occasion for wild enthusiasm. Electric cars, hidden in the thickets, illuminated the stage all night, while in another grove, forty musicians, under the direction of the conductor Desportes, played the precious music of Bach, Lulli, and Boccherini.

When the spectacle began, at the very moment when Bacchus came on to the stage with Silenus and his ass, we feared it was going to be interrupted by a torrential downpour. A shower began. I had been warned of this menace by the Observatory of the Tour St. Jacques, which foresees everything.

I went on to the stage, and with a gesture I calmed the dismay of my guests. On the very instant, the rain stopped, and everyone believed Jupiter had commanded the elements. Then, when the performance was over, the guests wandered through the forest, until supper was served as the first rays of dawn appeared. At four o'clock in the morning the twenty maîtres d'hôtel laid the tables in front of the Pavilion of Ange-Marie Gabriel, on that side where it is surmounted by a pediment by Coysevox, representing a boar hunt. Accompanied by twenty nymphs they filed among the little tables around which the guests were grouped, bearing on their heads or their shoulders the splendours of a supper Vatel would not have disowned; 300 melons, 300 lobsters, 300 *foie-gras*, 300 ices, etc. . . .

Isadora Duncan was near the master of the house. Drunken with wine and with the splendour of the scene, as much as with the popularity she enjoyed in this gathering of artists, she climbed on to the terrace which was the stage, made the orchestra play an aria by Bach, and interpreted it with her unforgettable genius. Jupiter, unable to resist this suggestion, mingled with her measure, and all saw him dance as dance the gods. It was a delirious improvisation that lasted only an instant, and I have been told that certain of the guests were moved to tears at so much beauty come together. It was seven in the morning before the 'buses, the Renaults and Voisins, deposited in Paris the half-unclothed nymphs and their slightly rumpled gods.

A little while after Isadora Duncan thought of returning me the compliment I had paid her, by displaying her before all the assembled artists of Paris. She organised a fête of the same kind, a Greek fête also, and asked the whole of the dramatic and artistic world of Paris to her studio at Neuilly. I went there with my wife, without knowing of the signal honour that had been planned for me. When Isadora had seated her guests, there remained only a table with two places, in the centre of all the others: she took one chair, and offered me the other. I was a little embarrassed by this predilection, and a little confused by being thus singled out; it seemed to me that this favour was out of place, but I had neither time nor means to reflect about it, in the proximity of this Bacchante who drew me to her and insisted upon champagne and kisses. As the supper drew to its end it seemed to me that I had taken up before Paris responsibilities of the most compromising sort – all the more as M. S. appeared unexpectedly before our little table, in his Greek costume over which was a very modern overcoat. Then he said, turning to his sons:

'Which of you is coming home with me? There's no longer any place for me in this house.'

That was forcing me to take up a definite attitude. I judged it not incumbent upon me to reply to the provocation, and I effaced myself while Isadora Duncan said au revoir to him with considerable affectation. Then everyone danced, and above all, She danced, magnificently, marvellously, divinely, as only She knew how. In front of the vast mirror in her studio one saw a small silhouette, for a long time immobile, developing the slow and formal gestures of a sorceress spreading around her every seduction, every philtre of dreams: accelerating her movements from minute to minute, she precipitated the rhythm of her incantation to the point of exhaustion in wild whirlings, and finally fell to the ground as if in final overthrow. How many times had I, elsewhere, seen this spectacle without experiencing the slightest sensation? Isadora alone has expressed the grandeur and the poverty of this theme, and she did it with a greatness of feeling that won to her everyone who saw her. She had to go to her room to rest awhile, and refresh herself, after the effort she had just made. She was still there at three in the morning when M. S. entered like a thunderclap. The greater number of the guests were still in the studio, sitting talking in little groups. I can see in my memory Mme Cécile Sorel, Mme Rachel Boyer, Mlle Marie Leconte, Mme Desti, Van Dongen, Mme Jasmy. I was near the door in a dark corner – as a matter of fact I think it was dark everywhere. 'Where is she?' M. S. asked tersely. Someone answered him that she was in her room; he went up to it raging, and found his friend in close conversation with M. Henri Bataille. He left without saying a word. I was relieved of a great weight.

I feel very much at my ease in relating this little scene for, despite anything that has been said, thought, or insinuated, I never had any but friendly relations with Isadora; but she held a very high place in my heart. We had several times held communion in the sacrament of beauty. One day, when she came to ask me to go to one of her concerts, she found me very much affected by the loss that had just occurred of my best collaborator, who was also a friend of whom I have spoken in the preceding chapter, M. Rousseau. I said to her that I was too sad to go out. She insisted that I should come, and gave me the big box in the middle of the hall, so that I could sit at the dance with friends who had known my faithful Rousseau, and she added:

'When it is finished, don't go. Stay in the hall, and I will dance for him.'

After the customary applause – she was acclaimed thirty times over, for the electrified public could not tear itself away from the charm of the idol with whom it had just been in such close communion – she maintained and kept up the flame of their enthusiasm by appearing now with a bouquet of marguerites, now with a single rose, now with a kiss full of meaning and expression. Finally, the crowd melted away. I remained alone with my friends in the vast amphitheatre of the 'Trocadero' in which the most glaring lights had been extinguished. She had asked Maître Diémer, who was there, to sit at the great organ and play, as only he could, Chopin's *Marche Funèbre*. My heart swells almost to bursting when I recall what I saw on that evening. Someone must have described somewhere Isadora dancing, and explained the miracle. She came up as if from the earth, as if she were being born, gave herself up to a disordered, pathetic, rending, and most human mimicry, and then fell back into the void with a majesty and gentleness beyond my power to express. With tears streaming down my face I threw myself into her arms to tell her the profound joy she had given me, and how proud I was to have offered so solemn a mass to the memory of my friend. She said to me simply: 'It is the first time I have danced this *Marche Funèbre*. I never dared to do it. I feared lest it might bring ill fortune upon me.'

Less than a fortnight after, she lost her two children, in a very horrible accident.

I had occasion to ask her certain æsthetic advice. She received me in her intimacy, to initiate me into her studies, particularly at Bellevue, in the palace which is to-day the Ministry of Inventions, in which she was then working with Walter Rummel. One day she asked me what was, in my opinion, the most characteristic intelligence of our epoch. I don't think I was qualified to answer her, but in the glow of conversation I cited several names, and amongst them that of Maeterlinck, one of whose recent books I had just read. She explained to me that she dreamed of making a child who should have the architecture of Isadora and the genius of a poet. 'I make children very well indeed,' she said to me, 'but I need someone who can give them an intellectual flame as beautiful as their physique.' I had the discretion not to follow the matter to its conclusion, but it was reported to me that she had proposed the matter to Maeterlinck, who had taken refuge behind his conjugal situation. It was added that she had sought out Mme Georgette Leblanc, to ask her to raise her veto. I know nothing of this, except that one morning Isadora appeared at my house, radiant, and said: 'Poiret, I have a fine child, as big as this,' and with her two hands, she indicated an exceptional size.

I had pronounced a name: that of Maeterlinck: but I had thought of the name of another, and I had only prevented myself from saying it because I knew his tastes and inclinations. I could not picture Max

Jacob in Isadora's arms. But would it not have been curious to have seen a son born from this amphibious Breton archangel, whose wings have cast a shadow over all the young of our epoch? Max was a charming friend to me, and I still often caress the book he dedicated to me, and which one day will be recognised as one of his finest works, when the public has freed itself from nebulous influences. It is the 'Cinematoma.'

Life set us on different paths. We have neither the same tastes nor the same beliefs, for to-day he is more Catholic than I am, but I keep for him a tender memory and a pious admiration, despite the blows and wounds we continually exchanged. He is the Man-Paradoxical who is ever struggling between two extremes, and whose soul is ever tugged by two complementary and rival forces, God and Satan, Black and White, Vice and Virtue, Water and Fire, Rome and Jerusalem.

I was already his friend when he saw Jesus appear in his room in the Rue Ravignan, and I listened meditatively to his revelations of the symbolic and mystical significance of the blue trimmings on his yellow robe.

One day Max asked me to let him give in my salons a lecture on the symbolism of St. Luke that, according to him, would interest all Paris. I had six thousand invitations printed, whose envelopes he wanted to write himself, for he desired to address only the great of the earth. All Paris was informed. Thirty people troubled to come.

XIV
The War

I have always detested the military, less because of the bad treatment they have inflicted on me than because of the amount of time they have made me waste. Consider that with the war, my compulsory service, and my training periods of twenty-eight days, I have been a soldier nearly six years, and during the best years of my life. And then, I have a critical mind, and then, I am more accustomed to command than to obey, and then, I have always found the military second rate and inadequate, even in victory. None the less, I love my country, and I have sometimes wept on beholding the flag.

So the reader will not find in these pages that martial pride that might be thought becoming to a soldier of the Great War. I played in it, alas, a mediocre and very minor rôle, brightened only by comicheroic adventures I will now try to relate.

Two months before the war I was in Germany, where I was undertaking a commercial tour. It was there that I received the order to return, instructing me to take part in a period of military instruction. I went to the French Consul in Cologne, and asked him to inform the War Office that I would not be back for a month. That is what one has to do in such a case. He promised me he would do it, but did not. Doubtless he had other fish to fry at that time. When I returned to Paris at the beginning of July I received a visit from two individuals of highly characteristic appearance, who asked to speak to me privately and confidentially. As soon as we were alone one of them told me that he was the bearer of a warrant for my arrest and bringing out from his pocket some papers:

'I have therefore come to arrest you. I presume you will not raise any difficulties.'

I shouted with laughter in his face and told him that I did not feel myself guilty of any misdemeanour but that, although *sans peur et sans reproche*, I would consent to come with him, on condition that he took a taxi at my expense.

A quarter of an hour later we were at the *Conciergerie*, where I was measured from head to foot, and my photograph and description taken, as also my finger prints; these formalities accomplished, I was taken to the *Invalides*, to the headquarters of the Military Government of Paris, where I was shut up with those arrested for insubordination.

My comrades were far from reassuring in looks, and the *gendarme* who bore the great key of the door would not take the responsibility of the ten thousand francs I happened to have on me. So he said: 'I have no drawer that locks with a key, and as I don't want to keep the money I will tell the Governor.' He sent an orderly, and a quarter of an hour later the door opened to let me out, amidst the grins of my new comrades who thought, looking at my straw hat and yellow shoes: 'Another gent with influence.'

The Governor's representative was astonished to see me, and thought my arrest was the result of a mistake. He offered to set me free provisionally, on the express condition that I would give myself up at his first summons, which condition, of course, I accepted.

I left the same evening to rejoin my family, who were on holiday at Kerfany in Brittany. I had hired the three villas and even the hotel, which comprised the whole hamlet, to be certain that I would be alone there with my guests, and free from the importunate. I had with me a family of Viennese artists, and the writer Roger Boutet de Monvel, the brother of the great portrait painter.

I was beginning to benefit from my holiday. One day as I was coming back from fishing in the sea, with a miraculous quantity of skate and lobsters, I was told that Jaurès had been assassinated, and that it was feared mobilisation might take place that afternoon. After lunch I went to the neighbouring village, and at the moment I arrived the tocsin sounded.

The peasants delayed not to come in from the fields; their forks over their shoulders they called to one another as they came up: 'Very well then, we shall go and see him, Wilhelm.' The women wept at the doors of their cottages. The chemist and the mayor, with M. le Comte de Beaumont, discussed matters in low, grave voices.

On my return to my villa I had my baggage and car got ready. I had to start that very evening. I said to my Viennese friend that I was going to take him to Paris with me. He said his bicycle was out of order. 'It is not a question of that,' I answered him. 'Austria has declared war on France. We were friends yesterday, we are enemies to-day. I cannot, I, a Frenchman, go to war against Austria, leaving Austrians in my house. I am going to take you with me, and you will be the first prisoner inscribed on the lists.'

I brought him to Paris, looking after him, but placing him beside the chauffeur, and next morning I gave him up to the military government, who shut him up.

Then I donned my uniform and said good-bye to my business, which was closing down for an indefinite period, and my employees, whom I left without work. Many of them accompanied me to the station weeping when I left to join my Corps. I arrived at Lisieux and I gave my papers to the corporal who was receiving reservists. 'You have defied orders,' he said to me. 'Fifteenth company, the building on the left.' I protested. I had not defied orders. The matter was being investigated. There must be a letter from the Consul, etc. . . .

'I don't care a damn. You are listed as having defied orders. Fifteenth company, building on the left.'

In the fifteenth company I met all the lawbreakers of my year, that is to say, low thieves and swell mobsmen, all the suspicious and equivocal characters, the outlaws. I was not proud. We were put under observation, and we were not sent into the firing line straight away, for they doubted our loyalty, and the manner in which we might behave.

On the next day the whole regiment assembled to leave for Charleroi, where the big German push was expected. My heart was heavy at not leaving with it, but the fifteenth company was kept back under observation.

A few days later my regiment was mangled. I lost the greater part of my former comrades. I saw a few come back, broken and wounded, in the first ambulance trains. Without knowing it the Consul in Cologne had perhaps saved my life by his negligence.

My description labelled me 'Tailor,' so I was employed by the regimental tailor. He was astounded that I didn't know how to sew, and took me for a stubborn, embittered fellow.

I had the luck at Lisieux to come across two friends whom I appreciated very much. The first was Eschmann, who, because of his physical condition, suffered greatly from military life. I have said that he was a delightful talker, whimsical to the last degree, who would leap from one subject to another with irresistible suddenness. I suggested he should share my modest room at a hotel. We dined in the evening with Derain, the famous painter, who was a cyclist, and we had the consolation in the midst of this life of hardships and threats of sometimes being able to take flight towards the arts.

We lived in the Hôtel du Maure, an old inn where I had to have my room repapered to get it clean. I put in a tricoloured paper which reminded me at every moment of what I had come to do there. I have let myself say that the proprietor of the hotel still shows it, as if it was the room of Bonaparte himself . . .

It was in this memorable but miserable room that Derain undertook my portrait. I did not want to be painted as a soldier, the costume being very little to my choice. I put on civilian clothes, and he devoted himself to revealing my character which, it seems, is despotic and Venetian. He did a very fine portrait, which I jealously preserved until the day when financial cataclysms obliged me to part with it. On the following day, encouraged by his example, I did Eschmann's portrait.

After this I presented to the equipment department a new model for the capote, of which I was the inventor. Its manufacture required 60 centimetres less than the official model, and saved four hours' work. I was taken to the Minister to submit my creation to him. M. Millerand was at one end of a vast table, surrounded by all the generals and heads of his ministry. I was able to explain to him the advantages of my new model in spite of the generals, who were shocked at my freedom, and tried to silence me by saying: 'You have not been questioned.'

Millerand gave the order to send me to Bordeaux, to organise there the industrial production of this new type of uniform.

I engaged some of my former workers to follow me, and I promised to guarantee them their living costs for a time, until the thing was going, and they could live on their emoluments. For three months I kept them at my own cost. I had been at Bordeaux for two months, completely unemployed despite my impatience to make myself useful, when I went to see Clemenceau, and told him that I had come to make military clothing, but that I had not been allowed to begin; that there was a disused church which might be made into a marvellous factory, that there were 3,000 women without work who might become dressmakers, and finally, that at Angoulême there was a depot of German sewing machines which might be used with advantage. Twelve thousand capotes a day could be produced, and they were needed.

Clemenceau thanked me for my communication, but complained to me that the Cabinet would not take any notice of him; and that he was put on one side and given no consideration, and he could not promise to aid my cause. He would nevertheless have a note sent to Millerand. On the next day the Commissariat officer under whom I was suddenly thought of giving effect to the conversations in Paris.

'How far have you got with your new capote?'

'I await your good pleasure.'

'A notice must be drawn up. Do you know how to draw up a notice for the *Bulletin Officiel*?'

That was not my way of making garments. I did not know how. Not without showing some contempt for my ignorance, he himself drew up a note addressed to all the tailors of France and of Navarre. It was a ludicrous document, in which one read *that the buttonhole of the side of the capote must be orientated according to the bisector of the angle in such sort that its projection would meet the last buttonhole in front*, etc. . . . This idiocy was sent to the regimental tailors in every district, and each corps replied telegraphically that it did not understand the new instructions. I was therefore sent, in my own car, first of all to Marseilles, to assemble all the tailors of the region and show them my new model capote, and explain the way to make it. I took with me the collaborators I had kept, thinking I might find them work and employment.

I arrived at Marseilles one morning, and at the Porte St. Antoine I was arrested by a group of detectives, some in civilian dress, others in uniform. We were all made to get out of the car and taken to the neighbouring police station. There they telephoned to the Special Commissary and the first words I heard were: 'We have got them.' I jumped and asked what that meant. 'You will soon see,' they answered me, and, escorted by a detective on each running-board and another beside the chauffeur, we were taken to the head bureau, to be interrogated by an aged dug-out colonel.

'As man to man, my fine fellow,' he said to me, 'what corps do you belong to?'

'The third Rouen Corps.'

'Then will you tell me what you are doing here?'

'Nothing simpler, I will tell you,' I answered calmly.

'That's it, in your own interests, tell me the whole truth.'

'First of all, I would like you not to consider me as an arrested person, but as a soldier who is in the process of accomplishing his duty. I am sent to you by the Ministry.'

He burst out laughing.

'What Ministry?'

'The Ministry of War, naturally.'

'Take care what you say. I am going to telephone to Paris, and find out if it is true.'

'It is to Bordeaux that you must telephone. The Ministry of War has retired there.'

'Would you first of all let me visit your car, and show me the cases of explosives?'

'I do not understand.'

'Yes, you have cases of explosives. Where are they?'

'I haven't got any, I don't know what all this means.'

'Would you like me to send experts to search?'

'Yes, if you like. I have nothing to fear from their expertness.'

Then two experts came and spread themselves on their backs in the mud, and when they got up they said: 'There is a case of explosives.'

I couldn't make it out at all, and I was wondering whether I were not the victim of some machination, when my chauffeur explained to them that it was the back axle, which was placed very low in this new Renault model.

The Ministry was telephoned to, and confirmed that I had really been sent officially by the Commissariat. It was urgent to assemble at once all the clothing manufacturers, and for me to address and instruct them. The Colonel's tone instantly became honey. He called me 'Monsieur,' and since it was noon he sent me out to lunch with my employees, asking me to come back at three. But as I was passing the corner of the Cannebière I was stopped by a policeman's signal; he took out of his case a small notebook in which he looked up something; then he said in a low voice to a colleague: 'It is them,' and he asked me to follow him to the Special Commissariat. On the way he told me that I was being watched for all over France, and that the order was to fire on my car if I didn't stop at the first summons.

After endless argument and explanation, I was released for the second time, but it was four o'clock in the afternoon before I was able to go to lunch. At six o'clock I was back at the Military Command with the Colonel:

'This is your way of being punctual then?' said he.

But I explained to him that I had been once more arrested. He promised me to give counter orders, and have it telegraphed throughout France that my person was taboo.

The tailors' meeting took place. Everyone seemed to understand my instructions, and I received an order to go to Limoges where I repeated the same operation, not without having been arrested once again at some railway level-crossing which had not yet received the counter order. From Limoges I was sent to Cherbourg.

As I was going through Rennes, I was near my family, which was still in Brittany; I asked headquarters for permission to take my wife with me in my car during the two days I was to spend in the district. This was granted me. The weather was horrible. My wife had a great yellow cloak and boots to match. We stopped at Coutances, to look at the façade of the cathedral. A *gendarme* took the number of my car, and at Cherbourg I received an order to rejoin my corps instantly, because of my conduct at Coutances.

Later I wrote to my superior to know what sort of misdemeanour I was charged with. He told me that a secret report from the *gendarme* at Coutances had reached the Ministry.

I then found myself, as the result of what circumstances I don't know, demobilised for two months. I profited by this interval to work at a subject that was scarcely familiar to me: military administration. I passed my examination, and was appointed an administrative officer of the third class. I was posted to the General Stores at Vanves, and from there to that of Rheims. I made the acquaintance of all the great producers of champagne. I lived in the Rue Chaude-Ruelle, in a little house which was the property of an ex-cook from Paris married to an old gardener. I found pretty flowers and good cooking, but the barest of rooms. There I received some of the great names of Champagne, who came to savour Mother Simon's mushroom pies, and presented me with the rarest bottles in their cellars. I also visited my friends in the Camouflage section, who were artists, and it was a pleasant distraction to dine with them. One evening when we were walking on the hills at Epernay, at the time of year when they smelt very good from the vine flowers, we were observed by an Austrian aeroplane, which aimed at us four bombs of the heaviest sort. We had only our fountain pens and brushes to defend ourselves with, and we returned to our dug-outs.

The bombardment of Epernay had begun. One had to sleep in cellars, on the ground or on mattresses, with the whole population. One could have believed oneself living in the days when the first Christians said Mass in the catacombs. One morning as I came up from my subterranean retreat, I had the surprise of perceiving that Mother Simon's roof had been smashed in by a shell.

Sometimes I was sent to Rheims to carry out grotesque missions. As I was given nothing else to do I considered them as a diversion. One day, for instance, I was sent to visit all the haberdashers of the town, to see if they still had any thread and buttons. I had not been to Rheims since its mutilation. I was horrified when I saw it, – it was a mass of debris through which it was impossible to progress: famished cats wandered through the desolation. I advanced a short way amongst these ruins, where there could be no question of finding any haberdashers; it was utterly impossible. The Germans who saw me from their lairs did me the honour to shoot at me. It was my baptism of fire. I was disagreeably impressed. I threw myself into a hole which led to a gallery, and the gallery to a corridor, and the corridor to a vault that was the cellar of Veuve Cliquot. There I found forty merry Frenchmen at table amidst hams, bottles of champagne, and candles. M. Werlé, the master of this house, which on that day seemed to be the château of some boyar, made room for me at his table, and asked me to choose the wine I would like to drink. The pipes that had formerly drained away the water were broken, and the cellars were flooded; one went about in a boat wangled by an oar, amongst the barrels and the casks. I wandered as if in Venice amidst these riches, and there filed by before my boat the most famous years of Rheims. But I stopped before a case of Calvados 1804 and a *fine* 1806. I took out two bottles. The lunch was sumptuous, we sang old refrains and ribald couplets. It was a sort of daily feasting, held by these men who at each moment were exposed to death.

At five o'clock we were informed that the bombardment had ceased. When I returned to the surface of the earth I found I was completely drunk. And in my pockets I found sixteen corks of champagne bottles. Had I drunk them? Fortunately I had an hour's journey in an open car in which to sober down. I returned to Epernay, and presented a report about the departed haberdashers.

I was to end my days as a warrior at Clermont-Ferrand, where I was sent in 1917 to direct great workshops for the cutting and making of uniforms. I was received by an administrative officer of the first class, full of importance, very sure of himself, and apparently proud of his Toulouse accent. Diplomatically I made him a few compliments about the importance of his stores and the good order that seemed to reign throughout his administration.

'Alas,' he said to me, 'it is a tremendous business, and a heavy responsibility. Tens of thousands of francs pass through my hands every day, and naturally, with such a flow, errors sometimes occur . . . and M. l'Intendant-Général will not understand that it is impossible to avoid them.'

'But that is very natural,' I said to him seriously.

'He makes me responsible, and insists on the repayment from my own pocket of any sums that disappear . . .'

'Really . . .'

'In my last monthly account there was a deficiency of six thousand francs, whose destination it is impossible to discover. I must either find where those six thousand francs have gone or else make them up from my own poor pence, which is not easy. I must borrow them.'

'Quite . . .'

'I must find some Crœsus who, without embarrassing himself, can lend me this money, which I would repay him little by little, in six months, for instance. You don't know such a person?'

'At first sight, I can't think of one . . . especially as I have just come from Paris and I don't know anyone in Clermont-Ferrand . . .'

'But there must be some comfortably off man who would not decline to help a comrade . . .'

'Crœsuses are becoming more and more rare. I, who am not a Crœsus, am not as rich as I am kind hearted, and in spite of all my desire to help a friend . . .'

'Well then, I take you at your word, and if I need anything, I will permit myself to tell you, as a comrade; I thank you for your gesture, which I shall not forget, M. Poiret.'

I was most depressed by the turn the conversation had taken, and furious about this misunderstanding. The very next morning he came to my office and led me to the town square where, before the statue of Vercingetorix, he cordially touched me for an *apéritif* and six thousand francs. In exchange he gave me IOU's for an equal sum, the first of which fell due six months later.

In my work I had every conceivable difficulty and obstacle to surmount. I had over me a sick man who was the most troublesome officer in his service, and known all over France for his incisive and subtle malice. I wish I had kept the pointed and poisoned notes which he continually loosed at me, to give you an idea of his cruel and hateful character. Happily the end of the war was approaching. My only thought was to reach it without getting myself into some bad entanglement. I did everything possible to avoid a collision with this individual who, for his part, sought a pretext.

When demobilisation was discussed a note was sent to every staff stating that certain officers might be considered indispensable, and kept at the head of their departments for a few months longer. As my captain could not repay me he feared lest my departure should give me the opportunity of demanding his delayed instalments. I was thus inscribed as indispensable, and on this account kept after the date I expected. I solicited an interview with the Intendant-Général, and told him my astonishment that I had been granted the title of indispensable, when I had been the object of every reproach and every outburst from the Intendant B——, who had said that I was of no value in my work. This opinion about me was surely incompatible with the claim to keep me as indispensable . . .

The logic of my reasoning appealed to M. l'Intendant, who was very correct, and said to me: 'M. Poiret, I understand your haste to resume your place at the head of your customary occupations, but I will not let you go unless I obtain from you a promise that you will pursue your debtor . . .'

I did not know that he knew about our bargain. I promised him I would be rigorous, and I was able to depart, taking with me my 6,000 francs, and the opinion I have about the military gentry.

I had happened to spend several weeks in Paris to see about a French propaganda exhibition in Spain. The dressmakers had organised parades in Madrid and I had been summoned to determine the details. It was then that on two successive days my chauffeur was found guilty of two infractions of the law by the same policeman: the first for using his Klaxon, the second for parking in the wrong place. When my chauffeur told me the second time that he had again been found guilty of an offence, I came down from my office to interrogate the Draconian policeman, and I asked him if he had some old score to wipe off with my chauffeur, for it was impossible to be persecuted in this way; and I added something very military indeed.

From that moment, I was for it; the policeman, who was of the pallid and raging type, with glaucous eye, a sort of reformed thug, made a report to the military government of Paris. It was the time when the young airmen used to make the 'tecs jump by racing down the Champs Elysées: orders had been given that these modest functionaries must be respected. I was arraigned before a Court Martial; it did not occur to me to laugh at it, and I was appalled that so small a matter could take on such tragic proportions. My friend Peytel, a barrister, who had won the Legion of Honour on the battlefield, offered to defend me. When the moment came for me to enter the court, as the accused, dressed in my uniform and surrounded by sixteen soldiers with fixed bayonets, I thought I would die of shame.

But my emotion reached its climax when the Court Martial entered, and I saw that I was going to be judged by a negro colonel. In my confusion of mind I asked myself whether I was at the 'Vaudeville' or the 'Grand Guignol.' How was all this going to end? Would he have any inkling that there was a certain friendly connotation in the very frequently used remarks I had addressed to the policeman?

He showed that he was not altogether black, and that he had all the grace of mind of the Creoles. I was condemned to a fine of 50 francs. I would have paid a great deal more than that to have told that policeman just what I thought of him.

XV
In Morocco

I felt I could not get back to work without first resuming contact with some element of pure and revivifying beauty. I was very depressed by military life, and only my robust constitution had saved me from sinking into neurasthenia. On the spur of the moment I decided to spend several weeks in Morocco, before restoring life to my businesses – divided into three branches, dressmaking, perfumery, and interior decoration – which had all, in my absence, declined to the point of ceasing activity.

I will not give a travel diary about this land that has been painted by the Brothers Tharaud, and so many other talented writers. But there are things of which I must speak, because they caused the birth in me of states of mind whose influence I perhaps still feel. There are sights that etched on my mind such deep lines that my memory is still dominated by them.

Thus I shall always see in my mind's eye the gold-weigher with his Shylock's face in the Casablanca ghetto, gazing avidly upon the little weighing scales. His two grandsons, educated in some London college, young dandies in grey trousers, Eton jackets, and bowler hats, had come hundreds of miles to embrace his silky beard, and he, he gazed on his scales and did not let his eye leave them, until he had settled with absolute certainty the matter in hand. Then he turned round and placed on each young man a thin white hand. It was a characteristic family picture, a summary of Israel's great adventure through the world.

I went further into Moroccan territory. I knew the tragic, mystic Aïssaouas. When I was in Marrakesh it was like spending days in Biblical times. The Mamounia did not then exist, and the hotels were simple enough. I lived in a former palace, and my room was only closed by a curtain which the wind blew over a courtyard crowded with oranges and lemons, through which there gurgled continually the song of a little stream. I spent hours near the Bab el Khemis gate, and I wandered beyond the walls along the dried-up river, which still has enough water for sheep to be washed. It was the road that led to the tanners' quarter where, amidst the acrid stench of decomposition, I never ceased from admiring these copper men, so like the Egyptians painted or sculptured on the walls of some hypogeum. There I rediscovered the man with the wheelbarrow, the crouching scribe, and he who bears on his shoulder a lictor's rods, his feet set exactly one behind the other, the legs rigid, the glance direct, the neck perpendicular upon square shoulders. And there was also Tobias, and the Maccabee Brothers. I was stirred as if some accident had transported me to another planet, or to the first ages of mankind. A natural scene sandy and chaotic, with here and there the plume of a rickety but hundred year old palm, rusty dust, a golden mist, through which the camels and gandouras seemed vermilion spectres – everything worked together to make me homesick for a land and epoch where, perhaps, I had passed some previous life.

It was Fez that tore me from the grip of Marrakesh. Fez still, to-day, appears to me the most beautiful thing I have seen in this world. The evening when I arrived there (it was the day of Ramadan) a poignant emotion filled the whole populace. Everyone was waiting for the voice of the trumpet that would ring out at the same time from all the minarets in the town, when a certain star had appeared on the horizon. Would it appear that evening, as they hoped, or would it not be visible until the morrow? They fasted passively as they waited. I reached my hotel, situated near the Bab Ghissa gate, and I went up on to the great roof, whence I observed the whole rose and white city, built like an amphitheatre between the two hills that dominate and frame it. What peace! One heard voices one by one, distinctly, rising to heaven like vertical smoke. One saw as on a map the covered ways, the sloping alleys, among the roofs thorny with white minarets, whose peaks became rose and orange with the gradual decline of the sun: and this at first tender colour, that caressed all the tips of the mosques and houses, little by little became burning, incandescent. The town was like flowing lava, or copper fused in some gigantic crucible. But the crucible filled with mauve ash, and the flaming peaks went out. The sandarac covered over the brazier, and the daily repeated miracle transmuted all the tints, to drown them in a mauve and blue harmony that was night.

I was filled with profound contemplation and I could have wished to say unto Allah his favourite prayer in Arabic, when, suddenly, a few yards from me, from the summit of a neighbouring minaret, there crashed the thunder of trumpets of an unknown timbre, and from every part of the town copper mouths repeated the same joyful, delirious summons.

In the twinkling of an eye all the women of the town were on the roofs, in robes of sparkling rose and orange tinsel. They uttered sharp cries as they struck their lips with their interlaced fingers. Bonfires were lit on the roofs of the houses of the rich. Incense and olive branches were thrown into them, so that they should blaze more brightly.

For an hour the whole city was given over to clamorous sharp joy; it was like a vivid delirium tremens. Among the rosy bonfires there were to be seen everywhere miserable little green and blue fireworks, for they were the only ones allowed by the Explosives Commission. These luminous little snakes traced out fleeting arabesques over the town and burst noiselessly, inoffensive and childish. Then the crowd dissolved as suddenly as it had gathered and trickled away toward I knew not what invisible banquets, toward I knew not what mysterious and hidden intimacies. I remained upon the roof as if to prolong the ecstasy of the unforgettable minutes I had lived through. What was the phantasmagoria of a Thousand-and-Second-Night compared to this dazzling reality?

A further emotion awaited me next day, when I heard the tale-teller of the Bab Ghissa gate.

The walls of the town of Fez look out upon green and luxuriant fields, that are yet very much broken up. The Bab Ghissa gate opens on to the Virgilian setting of a cemetery-amphitheatre. Let us be clear about it: An Arab cemetery, where the tombs are flagstones level with the ground set amongst laughing, flower spangled turf. No crosses, no columns, no stelæ, but seats of earth or stone where families come to take tea in order to entertain their deceased relatives, and converse with them. Friends are brought, and little birds in cages, and the day is passed in warm and animated converse with the deceased. They sing, they clap their hands to mark the rhythm. These fields of the dead are full of white shadows that are the silhouettes of the living, contemplative and full of piety.

While this scene unrolls on the slopes of the hillside, caravans and flocks of cattle, sheep, donkeys, camels disappear beneath the town gate, silent and eurhythmical. Towards five o'clock the garden-cemetery fills with a denser crowd. With impressive calm all the men seat themselves on the unequal steps of this natural theatre, and patiently await one knows not what ceremony. When the shelves are filled with the multi-coloured crowd, in the midst of this verdant setting an old man with white beard steps forward and takes his seat, in a low place just at the foot of the town wall, which serves as a tympanum to his thin voice. Slowly he begins a gentle story, which will progressively become the most terrible cloak-and-sword romance one could ask of human invention. Now and again he hurls some dart or sally that unlocks a silent laugh through all the audience. Every mouth opens, every shoulder is shaken for a few moments. When calm returns, he continues. It is thus on every day of the year, and often in the afternoon, at five o'clock, I think: 'Now, at this very minute, the tale-teller of the Bab Ghissa gate has seated himself upon his seat, and is beginning to recite his tale in silence and in peace.' And at six o'clock I see them all get up together, with one and the same movement, when the voice of the muezzin, from the summit of the minaret, sends forth to heaven his strident notes, and summons them to prayer. I dream of living in my own country, a peaceable and ecstatic existence like theirs, and of melting into a perfect communion with nature, whose vision has always raised me above myself and above material things.

On my first journey to Morocco I had the honour to be received by Marshal Lyautey, in his former residence at Rabat – the new one, which he had undertaken but which he scarcely inhabited, was not yet finished. During lunch, the conversation turning upon general political conditions and the threats hanging over Europe, I said to the Marshal: 'If there were a wave of Bolshevism in France you would without any doubt have a wave of *Bourgeois* coming to Morocco, for the French consider that here they have a garden, and perhaps a place of retreat.' Then the Marshal, without a blink and with his terrible eye, barked at me:

'I would not accept everyone, and I would refuse the useless.'

'But all the same,' I replied, 'if the French wanted to settle here?'

Then the Marshal, opening his right hand and closing it again with a firm gesture, said: 'I have the natives in the palm of my hand.'

This but-little-Republican phrase pleased me immensely. It was the utterance of a leader, and I have always admired leaders, persuaded as I am that we lack them. We have only bosses, nowadays.

But I was not only received by the French authorities, I became the friend of the Pasha of Marrakesh, who always treated me as a *grand seigneur*. The sumptuousness of his receptions is well known. He has fifty-two cooks and, on gala days, each of them produces his own speciality. Did I not fear to plunge into culinary digressions I would describe that copper vessel in which I was presented with two hundred scrambled eggs. Those who have only eaten scrambled eggs in little European dishes ought to make the journey to Morocco to learn what a scrambled egg is, mixed with 199 others. There is also pastilla, which is a marvellous flat paste cake, as big as a small table, and inside which one discovers, by a thorough search with one's fingers, pigeons stuffed with sausage meat and frangipanni. It is a marvel. It is unnecessary to describe the *méchoui*, which every mistress of a house now produces readily. But I must say a word for the salad composed of a layer of fennel, a layer of orange, and a layer of chopped chervil, frosted with powdered sugar which appears before you like a wintry lawn and which, in your mouth, recalls all the gardens of spring and summer.

All these gastronomic treasures, the pride of Arab tradition, would be very little without the studied refinement that surrounds them. No hospitality is more distinguished; no welcome is more cordial and more courtly-refined than that of these little monarchs, who reign over populations of half a million. Motley and multi-coloured slaves hasten at their command, bearing on their shoulders and heads ewers and copper bowls and enormous silver cups. A whole mass is performed around the guests, who are assembled on cushions round a low table. A European cuts a poor figure amongst them, even when he wears his dress uniform. Ah, what would I have given to have worn, like my hosts, those superposed gandouras of white canvasy silks and mousseline-de-laine and butter muslin. The dark faces and live-coal eyes in the glacial coolness of their clothes are exceedingly disturbing, and the black fingers rubbing on the palms of their hands little balls of *couscouss* would be altogether too disquieting, if their nails were not at least as carefully tended as those of our diplomats.

The Pasha of Marrakesh, El Glaoui (which means 'The Mountaineer'), had welcomed me in the courtyard of his palace, where he was in the midst of dispensing justice. When he saw me, he suspended the session with a gesture, and came toward me with a full sweeping movement of the folds of his mantle, like a Tintoretto Doge or an El Greco Othello.

In the evening, he asked me to visit his own house, which was that of a great gentleman interested in the panoply of war; trophies, weapons, and armour. I went into his own room, where I saw a copper bed surmounted by a baldaquin with pillars, draped with rose silk muslin. Beside the bed on a little Louis Philippe occasional table, I found a dagger, a Browning of the latest model, and a fine shotgun, as if it had been the room of some gamekeeper in Sologne. I showed my astonishment in my face, and pointing to these objects I asked 'Why?' Then, with a sad and resigned smile, he said to me simply: 'I have brothers.'

Then he conducted me to his private garage, which was like a harem of pure-blooded automobiles. Hispano-Suizas, and Mercedes of the best years, were cheek by jowl with Voisins and Bugattis. 'Choose,' El Glaoui said to me. And from that moment one of the cars was mine, one of his chauffeurs having been placed at my service, with an interpreter beside him.

'Where desirest thou to go? Thou must surely go to Demnat, which is a pretty village.'

And I left for Demnat with my friends, going by tangled and desert tracks.

When we arrived at the outskirts of Demnat, covered with dust and sand, we understood what must be felt by travellers through the desert when they come to an oasis, – the first trees were more fresh and more shady than all the others. There were blue cedars, and oaks that seemed to us gigantic and hundred-year-old olives, and we were beginning to marvel at the mystery they spread about them when a cloud of dust came at us. Horsemen sent by the Kadi of Demnat came to greet us. After a brief exchange of compliments they accompanied us as an escort, skilfully carracoling against the wheels of our car. We arrived before the castle, which is like a feudal fortress; and the drawbridge was let down for us.

Our car stopped beneath a peristyle. Stewards welcomed us and the Kadi gave us the greeting according to the Mohammedan rite.

A great room that opened on to a courtyard planted with orange trees was opened for us, and in it we found a delicious coolness. Scarcely were we installed ere slaves brought us dishes laden with fruits and indigenous pastries. Others anxious for our repose brought us innumerable cushions. We let ourselves be carried away by the softness of the air, and our encouraging lassitude. Night fell with all the train of its benefactions. We slept.

But the heavy heat of the East, and its smells, prevented us from enjoying rest, and every moment we arose, either to listen to a bird singing a song new to us, or else to inhale the perfume of the oranges and tuberoses and pinks that streamed from the gardens and courtyard, as if the flowers had been crushed under foot. There was even a nightingale, which I believed was the bird *Bulbul*, taken from the Arabian Nights by my friend Dr. Mardrus, so learned was he in his vocalisation, and so utterly enchanting.

At dawn we heard regular vociferations that were like the voices of women, and which all came from the same point. We discovered a little staircase that led to a roof, and from there we could see some women, who had been condemned on the previous day to receive a certain number of whacks with a stick. The sentences were being carried out, and they uttered rhythmic cries, as if to measure exactly the duration of this mild torture.

XVI
Back in Paris:
The Oasis Theatre

I adored my garden, in it I passed divine hours, and I lunched there when it was fine. The table was laid in a retreat that permitted me to enjoy it without being seen by passers by. And in the evening I dined there, in the relative peace of Paris. I could have thought myself in some far off park, if it had not been for the noise of the traffic, and if there had been a little more oxygen.

I thought how I might let other Parisians share the delights of this oasis during the summer, and I pondered how I might provide in it subtle and refined entertainments that would appeal to the élite of Society.

First of all it was necessary to establish the framework of a theatre, and in order that it might function every evening, to shelter it from rain and bad weather. But can one cover over a garden, in which there are secular trees? One day when I was talking about it with Voisin, the great automobile manufacturer who is also a great inventor, and who never lets himself be held up by formulæ or routine, he suggested that a dome should be made out of the fabric used for airships. This envelope was double, it stretched over the whole surface of my garden, and sheltered it completely. Every evening a special motor filled it with compressed air until it became rigid. When this sort of carapace was completely swelled out, it formed a roof on which one could have walked; but it had no weight and it was easy to raise it on a tackle, and set it above the garden at such a height that one was not deprived of the sight of the trees.

The mere application of this discovery of Voisin's to an open-air theatre in Paris roused curiosity, provoked astonishment, and seemed thoroughly worthy of an innovator like him, and like me. Beneath this vermilion cupola, I placed spacious, comfortable, gaily coloured armchairs, in which one could enjoy a pleasant relaxation while lazily listening to the choice pieces I presented.

The first show opened with a lecture by Antoine. It was a false Antoine who, without any make-up and merely by the effect of a grimace or a contraction of his face, could imitate to perfection the appearance of the former director of the 'Odeon.' On the day of the first performance the real Antoine was there, and certainly he was not the least amused in the audience.

Having searched through every sort of collection for plays or farces of exceptional quality and curious interest, my choice fell upon Paul Reboux' and Charles Muller's *A la Manière de . . .* We played *Idrophile et Filigrane*, a Maeterlinck parody, and *La Triche*, a parody of a Henry Bernstein drama; and then there was that side-splitting fantasia of my friend Bain, called Bagnolet, which was entitled *Le Secret des Mortigny ou de l'amour à la honte, et vice versa*, interpreted by the Mortigny troupe, which was composed of painters full of whims, with a few professional actresses.

Another time we reconstructed the Parisian *Café Concert*, and the *Bals Musettes* of the last fifty years. La Taglioni, La Païva, La Patti, Lola Montès, and all the great hetairai of the Empire were to be seen, ghosts given their freedom in a reconstruction of the settings they moved in when they were twenty. The *Bal Mabille*, with its booths and refreshments, the *Jardin de Paris*, with its gas-lit slopes, were reproduced in their entirety, and all old Parisians were touched to their depths.

All the 'stars' who had made famous the most celebrated songs appeared on my stage: 'En Revenant de la Revue,' 'Les Pioupious d'Auvergne,' 'D'vant les Bains de La Samaritaine,' by Paulus – and Paulus was none other than René Fauchois, the great writer who, because of his striking resemblance to the famous 'star,' had consented, moved by his love of the art, to come every evening and give his turn in my theatre, which I had named the 'Oasis.'

One evening Paulus's son, having heard about this resurrection, came to the theatre. He wept, believing he was seeing his father again, and he ran to Fauchois, and embraced him in his dressing-room, so grateful was he for his fine rendering.

Theresa also was on view. She sang 'Quand les canards . . . s'en vont par deux . . .' or else, 'La femme à barbe,' or else 'La Patrouille,' from the middle of *La Corbeille*, that is to say, from the midst of the group of actresses seated in a circle round her, waiting for their turn to sing, with a bouquet on her knees, ogling the whole audience. It was the great singer Delna who played the rôle of Theresa, because of her baritone voice, which she made dramatic and comic by turns.

Here too Yvette Guilbert made her reappearance. I had great difficulty in persuading the great artiste to mount the boards once more. I had to implore her. To touch her heart and her pride I was forced to employ my whole repertory of arguments. She was sensible to those that resounded loudest, and she consented to repeat her former successes, despite her predilection for mediæval poetry, to the study of which she had given herself up.

Once again there were heard the saws of Xanrof, then *La Soularde, Le Fiacre*, and the youthful works of Maurice Donnay.

I had had a false Yvette Guilbert brought in, who imitated her far from well. Then it was that we saw the real Yvette stand up in the audience and say: 'Ah, no, Mademoiselle, your imitation is charming, but it is really not accurate. This is pretty much how Yvette Guilbert used to sing at that time.' And she would begin her number in the midst of a real ovation. The audience could not control its enthusiasm, and every evening she was repeatedly called back, and there were endless encores.

I also dug out the aged Bruant, who became my friend. I had gone to find him at Courtenay, in his retirement. He had a pretty house there on a hillside, where he lived with his wife who was Tarquini d'Or, once famous and still retaining the voice of her great days, although she has shared it with her son. I had never been to his house, and I had been given pretty vague directions as to the place where he lived, but before reaching Courtenay I saw some red chemises and scarves drying on a balcony. 'It's there,' I exclaimed, and I was not mistaken.

Bruant greeted me with embarrassment; he had not expected my proposition, and he declined it. The guarantee of a good figure did not move him. I had to double it. Even so, I left with only half a promise, but I counted on the intervention of Tarquini d'Or, who wanted to see Paris again, and the renaissance of her idol. It took place every evening, as regular as sunset. Bruant appeared in the traditional costume created by him, all in black velvet, with black boots, a red chemise and scarf, and an immense Rembrandt black hat. This getup gave him a grim, stern air, which was that of his songs. He spoke, in a voice that had grown no weaker, things that all the world had learned by heart, since his retirement from the stage: A *Montparnasse, A Bellevue, Le Côtier,* and *J' vends mon crayon pour un sou.*

This resuscitation gave matter for reflection to many, who had thought lightly enough of Bruant's transit across the Parisian sky, and who discovered rather belatedly that his work contained real beauty, and deserved greater consideration. I remained Bruant's friend; he was at one and the same time a great poet and a great *bon vivant,* a *brave homme* in the fullest meaning of the words, who still laughed at having been able to frighten the public and abuse the bourgeoisie at his own pleasure in his youth, making them pay for it all – those bourgeois of whom he had now become an example.

We sometimes dined together in a little Montmartre cabaret, with a few of his friends, and we would go up on foot to the famous hostelry, the *Lapin Agile,* where Bruant, naturally, was fêted by Frederic, the proprietor, and equally by the habitués. Despite the dim light which is the tradition in this castle of want, it was not long before the great chansonnier was recognised, and he was always begged to sing. He was pleased to be pressed, and to rediscover in the familiar setting of this innocent repair, and before this audience of the people that was also one of connoisseurs, the admiration he had always elicited.

At the 'Oasis' we also gave, each week, fêtes with different themes.

One time it was a fête of French Venery, to which all the guests were asked to come in hunting dress. Huntsmen in livery showed their red amongst the verdure of the trees and lawns. M. Boni de Castellane had made me outline the whole of one lawn with little deep green lamps, which blinked around the arabesques of carved box that marked out bowling greens. In the midst of this décor a real stag was propped up by branches, and a pack of hounds appeared with whippers-in. The kill was sounded, and the first huntsman of the Duchesse d'Uzes, who had lent her co-operation for the occasion, dismembered the beast.

The honours were rendered to the English Ambassadress. This rural ceremony in the heart of Paris, and but a few steps from the Champs Elysées – was not this a real surprise?

Another day the fête was called 'The Stomach of Paris.' All the guests in evening dress were given a blouse to wear as they came in, and a peasant's bonnet or a market porter's cap, and the setting was that of a village square on market day. The carts that descended the Champs Elysées full of carrots, turnips and cauliflowers were parked in the garden, and the vegetables were taken from them and shared out amongst the beautiful market women, who had been given shopping baskets. Everyone went off with the materials for his own stew. There was an open-air seller of fried potato chips. He was not idle, and spread about his own very particular smell, which completed the realism of the proceedings.

The feast of the New Rich was also a great success. All the women had to come to it dressed in gold or silver. That was insisted on. Louis d'Or and Thunes (five franc pieces) were thrown in profusion on to the dining tables, and golden rain and fireworks inundated the whole scene. Dozens of oysters were distributed, inside which were pearl necklaces. The theme of this party was all the more piquant because, precisely at that moment, there was widespread financial embarrassment, and the New Rich were threatened with the probability of shortly becoming Anew Poor.

There was also the fête of Moonlight, in which all the women became charming columbines, thanks to the trinkets that were distributed to them – feather boas, nets of pearls and diamonds, and white powder and crescent moons, while the men wore over their smoking jackets a pierrot's great muslin collar and flour-covered hat. An Arab prince, strayed into this, had pierrot's pensive gaiety and the melancholy of a black Virgin.

The whole garden had been covered with gossamer and silver beams fell from the sky like an impalpable rain, amidst a tender blue light.

Naturally the guests could not tear themselves away from these charms, and had difficulty in understanding that they had to go at two o'clock in the morning.

I had many bones to pick with the police, who raised a thousand difficulties in my way, and added their vexations to the natural risks of the enterprise. The 'Oasis' was a fiasco that lasted only one season, but I left behind in it half a million . . .

It was my fault. I ought to have known that at that time of year there were not enough Parisians to make such a venture prosper. As for the foreigners, who in the months of July and August constitute the clientèle of Paris, they could not understand the charm of the revivals to which I had devoted myself. Paulus, or Theresa, meant nothing to them. For this profane public Fauchois was unknown, and the *Bal Mabille*, presented by dancers who did not show their legs naked, had no interest for them.

At the end of the performance one saw the Empress Eugénie, surrounded by her ladies of honour, with their huge hats and ringlets falling on their shoulders, sitting in the park. It was the reproduction of Winterhalter's great picture, which is known and loved by all artists. While one part of the audience stood up to applaud this vision from history, the Americans went out, as indifferent to the Empress as to Winterhalter, in a hurry to get back to their cosmopolitan palaces, or to kick about in smart dancing places.

Bitter it was!!!

XVII
In America

I have several times visited America, and made certain observations that I should like to publish, but I fear to prick the amour propre of the Americans, which is, like everything concerning them, the greatest in the world. How many travellers have restrained themselves from saying their thoughts, knowing that there is no place in that great country save for superlative laudation and dithyrambic praise? Criticism, however slight, reservations however delicate, are scarcely tolerated. First of all, therefore, I must ask forgiveness from Americans and their ladies for the small smarts these pages will cause them. If they feel themselves too susceptible, let them not read them. Do not enter; this is a thorn-brake. But yet, there will be found here the savour of wild fruits, for I speak as I feel and I will not refrain from uttering the admiration with which certain aspects of America inspire me. The arrows I may let fly at things American bear within themselves the balm to heal the wounds they make, because they are those of a loyal friend, who does not seek to do them ill, or any hurt, but to show to them, discreetly, oddities about which they can laugh with me; and, anyway, a dressmaker can but give pinpricks.

Now for it!

First of all, I must point out that I was the first Parisian couturier to embark for America. That will astonish nobody.

I did not know exactly what I was going to do there, but I had a desire to make the acquaintance of that nation, which appeared to me full of energy, nervous, and always pregnant with some new thing. What I saw of Americans in Paris was not enough to let me form a proper notion of what they were like at home.

I left on an October morning.

As I climbed into the train, I was given a copy of the *New York Herald* in which there was published a letter, or rather an injunction, from His Excellency Cardinal Farley, Director of the Catholic American conscience; a document in which this great prelate put all his flock on guard against the Demon of Fashion, which constituted a social and moral danger through the liberty, the licence, and the spirit of provocation of the creations of the designers of the day.

I felt myself pricked, for I considered myself the principal representative of the modern mode, or at least, the most conspicuous; but I knew, too, that my dresses were the chastest. I was then scarcely beginning to make shorter skirts, which stopped above the ankle, but I had, incidentally, brought with me a cinematograph film showing a parade of my mannequins in my garden in short dresses.

When I arrived on the other side of the ocean, before stepping ashore I was naturally surrounded by an army of photographers and journalists, who assailed me like mosquitoes. I had never encountered a like wave of curiosity and indiscretion. I was followed into every corner of the boat – sharing this honour with Polaire, the well-known artiste, who in America passed as the ugliest woman in the world – because it was in this way that her manager had secured her adequate publicity.

An interviewer more skilful and more dangerous than his colleagues asked me what I thought of Cardinal Farley's letter. I answered him with a thousand verbal precautions, for I saw the snare: 'His Excellency the Cardinal is right,' I said, 'and women's toilettes can be beautiful without awakening concupiscence. Outrageous décolletés are made to-day, but they are disapproved by people of taste, for the first quality of an elegant woman is to have tact, and a sense of proportion. French dressmaking rejoices to find the principles it has always professed echoed in the distinguished words of a prelate so eminent as Cardinal Farley. Furthermore, there is nothing to fear, for women have, at bottom, a solid Christian virtue, the resistant strength of which His Excellency must know; and if ever morality and coquetry were opposed, there would be heavy odds that coquetry would be defeated; isn't that so? But I am sure that the Cardinal does not desire to oppose them.'

A few days later I learned that my film, which had been left at the Customs for examination, had been forbidden by the Censor as obscene. I have often shown it since then, and each time I have asked myself what could have deserved this rigour, and what in this document of the History of Fashion could have shocked the Censor? If it was the short skirt, it must be stated that Americans have, since then, by far surpassed my hopes in the manner in which they have adopted it. I do not understand their custom of resisting so openly every suggestion of Fashion, in order to become as blindly its slaves, and to fasten themselves on to it furiously after a certain time, as if every new formula constituted a schism and an assault upon established order.

In Europe we have long recognised the instability of Fashion and of woman. We know that what is to-day a sine qua non of Fashion will be fancy dress in twenty years, and that to-day we consider ridiculous and grotesque the frock coats of our grandfathers. Soldiers alone escape this law of nature, in virtue of the august and venerated character of their functions. In an official military review in Paris uniforms of one hundred years ago were exhibited, and they did not seem costumes of light opera; but if they had been accompanied by civilian dress, the laughter of the public would have been as deep as was, in fact, its respectful contemplation.

One must not suppose that each new fashion is the consecration of a definite type of garment, which will replace for ever that which is being abandoned; it is simply a variation. As far as design in particular is concerned, it is a new æsthetic expression seeking to set off those charms of woman which have not been emphasised by the preceding version. For there are periods that forget to show the hair, others that hide the legs, others that bury the arms. Think of the leg-of-mutton sleeve. Is it not right that one should uncover, one after the other, all the beauties of the feminine figure, and that one should take pleasure in tracing them out?

Let us not forget that man is the only one of all the animals who has discovered clothing. And is it not his punishment that he is obliged to be continually changing it, and never able to find a fixed formula? He is the Wandering Jew of compulsive fantasy.

A creative dressmaker is accustomed to foresee, and must be able to divine the trends that will inspire the day after to-morrow. He is prepared long before women themselves to accept the accidents and incidents that occur on the trajectory of evolution, and that is why we cannot believe in a resistance by women, in their clubs, or through tracts, lectures, meetings and protests of any sort, against that which to him seems logical, ineluctable and already certain.

I remember the curiosity my wife roused on the boat when, on a rainy day, she appeared with boots of Russian leather. Are not boots a comfortable footwear for men? Why, then, should not women wear them, and why should they not be made yellow or red or green, for greater elegance? There is no logical impediment in this reasoning. One must be sunk in error if one cannot see it. And yet, everyone discussed Mme Poiret's boots . . . and photographers accompanied by journalists came to the Plaza Hotel, where I was stopping, to photograph the unforeseen and audacious novelty. I was considered the most daring dressmaker in Paris, but they had not expected that.

Two hours after our arrival, as I was sitting down to dinner at the 'Plaza,' I found on the table a newspaper with a photograph of the boots on my wife's feet. I became the man of the moment in New York. I was telephoned to during the night to tell them what colour were my pyjamas . . .

I was the object of all their curiosity, but happily not for long, for this favour lasts only a week, in fact until the arrival of the next mailboat, which brings to the pier a new array of top-liners, and in fact one must make haste to say what one has to say to the newspapers during the first week of one's stay, for after that, if one wants merely to correct a false rumour or an inaccurate statement, one has an antiquated air, and one is no longer heeded.

I had decided to come to New York at the instance of M. ——, a dressmaker of Fifth Avenue, who greeted me at the boat, and at once showed his intention of embracing me securely to him and arranging all my goings and comings. He bore me as a banner, draped himself in my dignity and made life impossible for me by monopolising me. I was obliged to foil his vigilance, and escape from the hotel before the hour he awaited me. I wandered alone about the streets where swarmed the people I wished to learn. I went into a shop where, by chance, I turned over a woman's hat, which seemed to be pretty, to find out where it came from; and I had the satisfaction of reading my own name; but there were also other very ordinary hats round it, and others again that were absolutely frightful. All bore the label of Poiret. I looked at the dresses that were hanging up on hangers. I might have thought myself at home, if the models had not been so poor, for all were marked with my name.

I tried to get a lawyer to take up my case; he took me to one attorney, then to the Attorney General of a district (I don't know if the titles are correct), but I was told, in substance, that this commercial proceeding was not prohibited by the American law, and that, in any case, it could only increase the splendour of my name by spreading it through the distant States of Wisconsin, Connecticut, etc. . . .

I am not yet comforted for everything of this sort I saw, in New York and elsewhere. I cannot here go at length into the question of counterfeiting. It has become a habit, an inveterate custom. I do not see how the mass of American workers who refuse to admit the right of artistic property are to be educated. Thus, my first experience of America showed me a certain side of commerce, which is perhaps restricted to dressmaking, but which deserves to be pointed out.

When I returned to France I created the *Committee For The Defence Of La Grande Couture*, which comprised all my colleagues, who were horrified by my report. Events have since proved that it was not superfluous to organise defences against counterfeiting.

Another thing which the American traders appeared to me to practise was to pack mediocre merchandise under a distinguished label. In that country they will have labels, and as they have no understanding of the value of objects, they go by the labels only. To sell common merchandise under the name of Poiret seems to them a happy and fortunate notion. Oh, young French business man who will one day go to America (you must go there), never trust your flag to anyone, and be on your guard!

I shall not stop to describe my astonishment at all the things I saw – which were pointed out to me with a legitimate coquetry: the life of the great newspapers, the works where the *New York Herald* is printed – it has 100 pages on Sunday and from 30 to 40 every other day (probably this figure has been surpassed since my first visit, and is now out of date). Nor shall I say more of my admiration for the shops I visited, of their theoretical organisation that is so nearly perfect, for example, Wanamaker's, which has a colossal turnover. It was at Wanamaker's that I gave a lecture on the occasion of a ceremonial parade of my dresses, in the great auditorium of the House.

This ceremony, which was attended by the cream of New York, was a real triumph for me. A few days after I repeated the lecture at Philadelphia, at the store of John Wanamaker. This great figure of American commerce who, in the course of a private reception, presented me to the great Redskin Chiefs in their gala costumes, explained that they were the oldest representatives of old America, while I was the youngest representative of the new Europe. Then he showed me a desolating picture which was, as if by accident, the largest in the world, and which occupied an entire wall in a vast room. I believe I recollect that it represented Golgotha.

You will believe me when I say that I appreciated as I ought the honour done me by Mr Wanamaker, the glory of the pioneers of his country, when he smiled on my young reputation, and had the 'Marseillaise' played each time I took a step. It would be superfluous to say that he was *au courant* with everything, and at every instant threw glances and mental bridges toward Europe, with all of whose arts and developments he was in touch. Everyone knows that, since he could not go himself to the annual exhibitions of painting and sculpture, he had the catalogues sent him from Paris, which he read avidly, marking with a red pencil the titles of the pictures he wanted to buy: *Retour du Lavoir, En Classe, Coucher du Soleil, Bruyères dans la Creuse,* etc. . . .

Most Americans profess a complete ignorance of the fine arts. In Philadelphia I have friends who are enlightened lovers and connoisseurs of modern painting, Mr and Mrs Speiser, and there are other celebrated connoisseurs whose welcome I cannot forget, like Mr Widener, whose salons shelter and preserve like tabernacles the rarest marvels of the whole world. I must also not forget the Barnes Collection, which is the finest monument of piety, the most beautiful altar that has been consecrated to contemporary art. But apart from a few initiates and monomaniacs, it seems to be true that the public at large are uninterested in all expressions of beauty. It seems, above all, that it is perfectly able to get on without it. It has no more need of statues in its gardens than of pictures on its walls, or of mirrors in its houses. For me, who live in a land where there are mirrors even in the street and between the shops, this seems extraordinary; where then can one analyse oneself, and control one's deportment and bearing, if one has not the aid of these constant witnesses?

I have often asked myself what is the origin of this indifference to all that makes for the charms, the decorations, and the distractions of life. I think the American has no time to give himself up to the fine arts and to the lovable things; his only preoccupation being to make a fortune. Money. That is the spring and cause of everything for him. The invention and convention of a work of art neither touches nor interests him. He wants things practical and positive, and has no desire save for the theatre, or rather the cinema, and that only so long as it is neither literary nor poetic, and represents everyday concerns. What attracts Americans in pictures is the price at which they can be bought and re-sold. Apart from their speculative value they are seldom considered, except abroad, when tourists have to kill time.

This disaffection for matters of art seems to me most grave and most distressing. They have a habit of saying: 'We are a young people, we have only existed for two hundred years, and artistic culture is beginning to germinate in certain strata of society; soon you will see. Wait.'

Wait for what?

Did the Phocæans, the Phœnicians, wait to cast their pottery, or blow into their glass the songs of their hearts, or to sow temples over the land and express by the working of materials their prayers and their emotion before Nature? The truth is that in America there is as yet no emotion before Nature, no sensibility, no national songs, no folklore, and that everything there is, to-day as formerly, borrowed from the foreigner. After two hundred years of existence, America brings nothing to the art of the world.

In all the lands whither I have gone, I have been welcomed by an indigenous intellectual élite of writers, painters, sculptors and musicians. In America, I saw no such people. But yet, forgive me, one evening some architects and decorators invited me out. They were giving a party. It was in fancy dress. I had with me some materials from which to improvise a fantastic costume. I went to the party; there was music and dancing. But they were Germans, who felt as isolated as I in New York, and were assuaging their home-sickness.

What can one say of the appalling Christmas and New Year's Eve nights, when one visits salons filled with shadows and mystery, without hearing any joyful songs, nor any wit, nor any freshness.

'What about Jazz?' I know an honourable opponent, who is well known to me, will say.

I stop him with a look.

'Jazz is not American, it is Negro.'

'But what about the skyscrapers, and Brooklyn Bridge?'

'Thank you, you provide me with my answer, for Brooklyn Bridge has not a single artistic detail. One of our architects would have thought of some useless detail which would have been put there for the sake of its beauty and decorative charm. Think of the Zouave on the Pont de l'Alma, of Sainte Geneviève de la Tournelle.'

But what is charm to an American? Everything is utility or necessity. They do not know how to invent the superfluous, the superfluous which, for us, is more indispensable than the necessary.

The American creates in a landscape whose dimensions are exceptionally great. One cannot, therefore, be astonished that their conceptions are vaster and more monumental than ours. When they stride across the Mississippi or the Colorado they cannot but construct immense viaducts, and are guided only by the necessity of reaching their objective, which is to bring two shores into communication. They would not let themselves be distracted from this end by any concern with decoration. Do beavers embellish their dams?

The architecture of the skyscraper has been created by necessities of a social order, which insist that a small area of ground shall return a great deal of money, and they must, therefore, be built up very high; and long-sighted police regulations forbid any cornice, any projection on to the street, etc., in fact, anything which is not a positive necessity. It is the very prohibition of decorative art.

Since we have uttered the great word, Prohibition, allow me to add that I regard this measure as also responsible for the lack of art in America.

With us there is an element which makes poets and stimulates all artists: it is wine. They have decided to suppress it. They will see what that leads to. What would Villon, Rabelais, Musset, Verlaine, Baudelaire, be without wine or any alcohol? And it was not only that which they themselves drank that enriched, enlightened and inspired them; it was that drunk by the generations of whom they were the descendants. The constraint the Americans have imposed upon themselves may have good results in sport and business, but will certainly not be able to increase the number of poets, musicians, or painters.

From the point of view of sport, my honourable opponent will say, the American race has achieved a great deal. I agree entirely. But is not sport very ill-suited to develop the artistic spirit? It develops capacities for work and a primary mental equilibrium, and perhaps it helps the play of the mental faculties; but in any case it does not favour that of the feelings, since it disciplines and regulates them. The whole education of the American, whether sporting or intellectual, appears to me to tend towards the control and oppression of this sensibility.

I am aware that the vast numbers of the population who must be ruled and governed, the masses that must be directed, impose on the Government simple and elementary methods of instruction and education, and that it is impossible to tolerate in a country of 120 million inhabitants licence or libertarian customs that might lead to disorder or perversion.

A land of 48 States cannot be managed like the Island of Tahiti, nor even like the little land of France. Its population must be canalised into rigidly straight channels, like the roads there, and protected from all risk of meeting with accident. It is very wise – but let them not say that they expect in the future a generation of æsthetes and lovers of art. They are scarcely being prepared for. There is no one to be seen in the museums, save, on Sunday morning, a few large families. And furthermore, there are museums that nobody knows, and if billionaire Mæcenases find satisfaction and a means of honouring the towns which saw their birth by building them, they are sadly disillusioned by the public's lack of interest. In New York, I asked twenty times over, in every class of society, for the address of an ethnographic museum, which no one was able to tell me. I discovered it right on top of Broadway, and I found nobody there. Baseball is decidedly preferred.

When one enters a museum, one must take with one a habit of mind which permits one to take interest in what one sees, and to retain and class one's memories. But I have the impression that in America what is acquired by the eye is not woven on a very active mental loom, for so many seemed content with a superficial receptivity, and did not try to derive further enjoyment from their sensations.

The teachers in the Art Schools, everywhere I went, seemed to me persons of infinite distinction, recruited from those European circles which are not always the best for the development of the minds of their pupils. German Protestantism, famous for its virtues, cannot reckon among them that of developing taste in the arts. I must tell you about my visit to Indianapolis, where I gave a lecture to an audience of more than three thousand pupils, who were studying for a career in the Fine Arts. I was most solemnly received by the Directress, white-haired and with gold spectacles according to the established formula, her right elbow in her left hand and a finger pressed to her forehead. She insisted so strongly that I must see the tapestries of the School that I looked forward to a real joy, and thought I should taste a true banquet of the spirit. I saw only a few gloomy tablecloths, especially that universally known one which represents Millet's *Angelus*.

If I am lacking in gallantry, it is in order to be strictly truthful, but believe me, I have no malice in relating these characteristics, which sketch, I hope, an outline of the American people.

I must also recount my meetings with various personages, for instance, M. —— who was called the 'Blouse King' and who, flattered at knowing me, offered me a mound of gold if I would let him have a monthly letter in which I would inform him of the evolution of the blouse in Paris.

This propensity of all their manufacturers to enter into contact with famous men in order to be able to appropriate their names and profit by them is an American characteristic. How many of them made me magnificent offers, in order to be able to give the name of Poiret to their merchandise.

One amongst them, who had set up as a manufacturer of shoes, made me a magnificent proposition: he would be authorised to use my name in his advertising and to print it on his luxury goods, in return for which he would give me $16,000 a year. I could not accept the bargain without seeing what kinds of goods it referred to. I therefore took the train with my manager, who had put me into contact with this powerful industrialist. We arrived at X—— where I was welcomed like a king by special envoys and Rolls-Royces. After the customary ceremonial formalities I began my visit to the factory, which lasted for several hours. I examined the footwear, which was intended for a clientèle of farmers: sturdy work-boots for them and their families. I could not think how the prestige of my name could have any relevance to this kind of product. I returned to the manufacturer's office where he awaited me in the midst of his heads of departments. He was wearing a suit in huge checks, and from his waistcoat pocket there emerged a cluster of fat cigars. I said to him:

'You can give me one of your fine cigars, for I have just saved you $16,000.'

'What do you say? How on earth—'

'By refusing you the permission you asked me, to put my name on your footwear. It would harm my reputation, and could not help you.'

You ought to have seen the faces of the heads of departments when they saw a man refuse, with a single gesture, $16,000 a year . . .

On my return a surprise awaited me. My manager, who could not be consoled for my free-hearted frankness, and would not admit that I was disinterested, demanded the 25 per cent I owed him on the contract, which had not been signed through my own fault; and I had to give it to him, all the Americans whom I consulted having supported his way of looking at it.

However, I did sign contracts with manufacturers, who made stockings and ladies' handbags and gloves, and especially, and now you will laugh, thread gloves! I had been asked to restore to fashion this article, which had fallen from use. I pondered long, and I found certain designs whereby interest could be revived in them if they were slightly modified; but these models were never put in circulation! I received my whole price but, to my astonishment, I was informed that my designs had not been understood, that they had asked themselves what was the use of them, and that they did not know the meaning of certain strokes of the pen or pencil. It was almost as if they had written to me: 'We do not know how to read.' But they had not written to me, for American business men never write.

Then I had a contract for ladies' handbags with a great firm, which did not keep its undertaking on the pretext that it could not understand my designs. An American has to see an article manufactured, completed, solid in front of him, so that he can copy it servilely. Their absolute lack of imagination prevents them from conceiving the unforeseen and the hypothetical. Like Saint Thomas, they only believe what they have seen. This must handicap them in science and in art, for it restricts their field of activity to the data of experience.

Knowing their inability to imagine, I thought of illustrating my lecture by practical demonstrations, and it was thus that I was brought to create dresses on the platform, during my last visit. First I would speak of Elegance, and I would try to make my audience's mouths water by rousing in them a taste for the new and the luxurious. Then, seizing the scissors in my pocket, I would unroll the multi-coloured velvets with which I was surrounded, and I would ask the audience to supply me with some lady who would be kind enough to lend herself to my demonstration. The whole audience would rise. I would then, after performing this little experiment, take a professional mannequin, who wore special underclothing in order not to shock the audience, which is always especially susceptible on this subject, as is known. For a few minutes I would drape and cut and tear away and pin on, and beneath my fingers, as of some skilled old witch, one saw born an evening dress, or a cloak. I could gauge the emotions of the audience by their 'Oh's' and stifled 'Ah's,' springing spontaneously from their breasts if I decided to make the sleeves in another colour, or some unforeseen facing that just set off the ensemble.

One day, at San Diego, near Los Angeles, I reproached my audience with being dressed almost in uniform: 'Look at yourselves,' I exclaimed, 'you all have a bouquet of flowers pinned in the same place on your fur. If it were a special and personal detail, it might have a certain charm, but when it is a general measure, I no longer look at it with pleasure; on the contrary, it grates on my nerves.'

When the show was over, the audience dispersed and I remained to converse with the director of the theatre. The man who swept out the hall came to me, and presented me in his apron with all the flowers he had gathered up under the seats. They had been sacrificed to my despotism.

On that day I understood the marvellous spirit of discipline which makes this population governable to the last degree, but which also causes its absolute want of originality. It is composed of 120 million school-children, who keep all their lives their childish attitude toward anyone who knows anything. But the danger is that they would soon become insupportable if, one day, they thought they knew more than their masters. That is what is happening in Parisian dress designing, on which they have sought to impose their taste, and substitute the experience of buyers for the inventions of creators.

A man who understands his craft, and who is a past master in his profession, does, nevertheless, dominate them, whether he uses a violin or scissors. I remember the sensation I created during my second visit. I was on the deck of the *Ile de France* with some artists who were going to Chicago. It is there that the highest fees are paid to all the Carusos of the world. There was de Luca, Major Formichi, and Mme Grace Holst Olsen, the great Norwegian singer, who told me she felt cold. I offered to go and fetch one of her cloaks from her cabin. She replied that she did not possess the sort of comfortable cloak she needed. Then, taking in one hand the scissors from my pocket (I always have them on me) and in the other my travelling rug, which was a pleasing Rodier plaid, I cut it, and improvised a cloak which was exactly what she wanted. The onlookers were full of enthusiasm. One of them must have telegraphed to New York, and recounted what he had seen, for on our arrival the journalists asked me to re-stage the affair of Mme Olsen's cloak – to illustrate the articles which were going to appear on the subject.

For the Americans, a little story like that is more important than a whole career given to the service of a great cause, for they are puerile, and boobies, and they believe everything they read in their newspapers. And that, of course, is what makes the incalculable force of publicity over there, while with us it is, practically speaking, negligible. The Americans lack the spirit of analysis and criticism that flourishes in the old world.

I don't want to launch myself out on a digression which would require a whole book for its development, but I think we are wrong to judge the Americans by comparing them with ourselves. There are factors of which we are ignorant. They have their élite of the mind, who have not yet crossed the water, but who perhaps one day will come to our shores. Writers like Sherwood Anderson, Dreiser, Sinclair Lewis, will soon become known in France. And one must say that the form of our education does not always make it easy for us to understand the mass of this people. On the contrary, it handicaps us, and our impedimenta of knowledge, culture and riches encumbers us as soon as we are on the boat.

The elementary schoolboy has a much better chance of getting into touch with and quickly adapting himself to this new environment. He can admire without any reservations the crowds rushing to their favourite shows, and the titanic advertising undertaken every evening by the commercial firms on Broadway, and the majesty of the Cyclopean architecture, at night crowned with searchlights: and when he had spoken his disgust, shared by all the world, for the abattoirs of Chicago, where assassination is practised in series, he will hasten to perceive that this daily crime feeds a Gargantua with one hundred and twenty million mouths, all gaping upon the same continent. What terror would be ours if Chicago ceased to feed this giant, and if the 120 million American appetites surged over the surface of the earth? Let us not hope for such a thing.

I was discussing these points the other day with a subtle man of letters, as I walked with him through the Versailles gardens designed by Lenotre:

'You must appreciate,' I said to him, 'the good things of America. Are not these eighteenth-century gardens kept up through the generosity of a Rockefeller?'

But my companion would not be mollified, and grumbled in his beard (for there are some obstinate Frenchmen), 'Timeo Danaos et dona ferentes.'

I should like to relate a few more memories of my travels in America, to tell some simple stories which are characteristic, and from which I shall not seek to draw any conclusion; it will be for you to do that, according to your nature.

I went to a boxing match in Chicago. What an amazing audience! Where had they been recruited, that evening? In all the seats, of which the cheapest cost five dollars, there were butchers and labourers of an inconceivable vulgarity and lowness; in the stalls one could recognise the nabobs only by their watch-chains and tie-pins, their rings and sometimes their bracelets, for all the spectators had the same scarred and patched up faces, in which glared savage, worn-out eyes. The floor was covered with spittle, and the atmosphere stank with cigars. Women were being sick all over the place, and boos, whistles and cries mingled in the sallow fog that bathed this dreadful festival. I have never witnessed anything so lamentable.

In New York, at the Ritz Hotel, they made one year, in a courtyard, a Japanese garden which had become the rendezvous of the elegant world. I was obliged to lunch there almost every day amongst the snobs. This Japanese garden appeared to me the very garden of idiocy and pretence. There is more intelligence in a penny fan in the smallest Japanese lacquered box, than in this courtyard, pompously garnished with cedars and little dwarf temples, amidst which ran an artificial river. A real Chinese woman sold cigarettes, and a Chinaman made coffee, without smiling, but perhaps not without suffering from so much stupidity. Nothing could have been funnier than the gravity of the staff and of the clients who, as they sat down to dine or sup in this setting, affected a certain distinction, and seemed to think that they were associating themselves with some manifestation of high art.

I know, of course, that one can lunch at the Speak-easies, but the formalities through which one must go in order to be admitted disgust and mortify me. First of all one goes in a taxi to the address which a friend has given one in a whisper, and one goes down a few steps as if one were going in through the basement of a house. Then the door does not open, but a barred peep-hole through which a page, or even the proprietor of the establishment, examines one and inspects one before asking who one is and who has sent one. When you have announced the name of your sponsors you are welcomed into a dark corridor, in which is the cloakroom. To the right or to the left you enter the dining-room, which, more accurately speaking, is a bar, and you order your lunch, consisting of frozen meat (as everywhere else) and vegetables cooked in water; and as you are in a house whose object is to escape from Prohibition, you ask for a bottle of Chablis for which you pay ten dollars. At the neighbouring table gentlemen who appear to be habitués of the bar delight in this programme; I am told they are members of the police. At every moment I expect someone will come in and exclaim, 'Hands up!' for there reigns an atmosphere of low suspicion that is incompatible with the name of these establishments, 'Speak-easies.' I breathe more freely outside, and I depart.

I was in New York on the night of the 1st of January and I wanted to give a dinner in my hotel to a few friends, and return hospitality. As a Frenchman I should have been happy to have had at my table a few bottles of good wine. I whispered to the head waiter, who suggested he should bring from his own apartment some bottles of Asti, which he had been able to obtain in exceptional circumstances. This complicity in receiving did not seem acceptable to me. I confided my wish to one of my New Year's guests, who then offered to procure for me three bottles of Pol Roger 1906 at the price of 300 francs each. After all, it was a whim, so why not? He brought them to me next evening when he came to dine, and we rejoiced over our crime, as we slipped them into a refrigerator. But at the end of the repast, when I saw the maître d'hôtel pour into the glasses a reddish and evil liquor I cried: 'Don't drink that – it is poison!' The bottles were brought to me, of which all the labels, corks and sealing had been counterfeited. It was a false Pol Roger for which I had paid 300 francs a bottle. I moistened my lips with it and found it undrinkable, but the Americans gulped it down, declaring themselves very satisfied, and I cannot think that it was out of politeness.

Seeing that I was alone in the hotel on such a great joy-day, my friends offered to take me with them to make, as is the custom, in that country, a nocturnal round of visits to their friends. In each house I found the same mysterious setting. The same veiled and shuttered lights, and in the penumbra, groups of men and women, the latter shouting with laughter, as if the men had said something funny. All drank unspeakable alcohol, inexplicable cocktails, and in the middle of the room there was a basin containing eau de vie cherries swimming in a criminal mixture. At times all the participants rose, spun about, staggered, finally danced. And they had an air of taking enormous pleasure in these gatherings which, to me, seemed amazingly insipid. Now, when an American says to me: 'We had a good time,' I know that what he means is 'I danced a lot, and above all, I drank a lot.'

In California I was the victim of the persecutions of the director of an important paper who wanted to compel me by any means to open a branch in his great city; he wanted to arrange for me the wherewithal.

Every day at noon this fat man came to inform me of the conversations he had relative to the project, and as he spoke he poured out for himself great potions of whisky, for he carried more than a quart of alcohol, having in each pocket a metal flask filled with spirit. This walking barrel naturally invited me to share his libations, but I rejected his offer summarily, for what he was drinking was positively infamous; and then, I wanted to disentangle what he thought from his jumbled verbiage, and I had to preserve my own clearness of mind. Sometimes he would say to me: 'I drink, you see, my dear Poiret, to keep this awful Prohibition law at bay – it is unworthy of a great people. I drink because it is forbidden, what pleases me is not alcohol, but the game of deception.' And a few hours later he would speak as follows: 'Why don't the Prohibition officers do their duty better? Why do we still find this frightful poison that degrades and debases us? We are like children, we don't know how to resist.' And, I don't know how, he would go home.

On my first visit I was invited by an important Canadian manufacturer to spend an evening on board his yacht on Lake Erie. I had to be in Buffalo next morning, and so we would cross the lake during the night. The dinner was perfect, of an utterly English correctness; we spoke little, ate little, drank still less, and amused ourselves not at all. When we came to the coffee, our host declared, turning to the ladies: 'These ladies will not be displeased to go to their cabins, for they must certainly be very tired after our doings to-day.' The ladies did not have to be told twice. They hastened to withdraw. As soon as they had turned their backs, all the panels groaned, cracked, and opened as in the romances of Alexandre Dumas père. Everywhere one saw bottles of champagne and liqueurs. With guilty looks the stewards produced Calvadoses, Marcs, Mirabelles, Kirsches, Scheidams, and Ratafias of great years. Without a smile my host poured me out innumerable whiskies until three o'clock in the morning, and when I returned to my cabin to go to sleep, he had a well-laced nightcap brought to me in bed; I had to throw it into the lake through my cabin's port-hole.

XVIII
My Lectures to
the Americans

I was constantly cross-examined about what I was going to do in America. People couldn't think what a dressmaker could have to say about Fashion. It is a futile subject which, by definition, seems to be incapable of analysis. None the less, I managed to demonstrate certain truths, which I tried to set before the eyes of a great number of Americans, and I wanted to make them know the fashions of France as they really are, and not as they reach America, adulterated, and filtering through unworthy intermediaries.

Here, chosen haphazard and presented without order, are a few extracts from my lectures, which may satisfy your curiosity. Let me add that my lectures were given in English, in great halls where sometimes there gathered seven or eight thousand female listeners. I cannot remember having met one man. Generally, I was welcomed with an ovation, after being presented by a chairman, as is customary in the United States, and I would express myself in these terms:

'I thank you, Ladies, for the enthusiasm you have just expressed. I know that you consider me a King of Fashion. It is thus that your newspapers entitle me, and it is thus that I am received everywhere, surrounded with honours, and fêted by vast gatherings. It is a treatment that flatters me, and of which I cannot complain. I must, however, undeceive you as to the quality of a King of Fashion. We are not capricious despots who, when they awaken in the morning, decide to bring about some change in habits, to abolish the collar or to make the sleeve swell. We are neither arbiters nor dictators. Rather we should be regarded as the blind servants of Woman, who, Herself, is always in love with change, and thirsting for novelty. Our rôle and our duty therefore consist in watching for the moment when She shall become tired of what she is wearing, so that then we may propose to her, at just the right moment, something else that shall be in

153

conformity with her wishes and her needs. Wherefore it is that I present myself before you armed with a pair of antennæ, and not with a rod, and I do not speak to you as a master, but a slave desirous of divining your secret thoughts.

'I am here only to serve you, and if for twenty years I have put myself at the head of every revolutionary and subversive movement, it is because the Fashion of to-morrow has always seemed to me more lovely than that of to-day. As soon as one Government is born, I dream of overthrowing it, to establish another which seems to me better; in this I am like our own old French Clemenceau. All my competitors, who are also inventors, would certainly agree that I am the most daring of them all, he who risks his reputation by enormously extending the limits of the possible, and who, every time, indicates to you exactly the point beyond which you would be going too far. It is as a creator that I wish to speak to you to-day, and I come to complain to you of the difficulty one has in interesting you in what is new.

'I have never met women more faithful than the Americans. That is not a fault, it is on the contrary a virtue, and rare enough, but when it concerns Fashion, this fidelity becomes routine, and routine is detestable. Fashion insists on change, and all creators complain of having to drag after their feet the fetters represented by the vast American mass.

'There are between you and us intermediaries whose function is to bring you our new ideas, and they do not perform their functions. They are sent to Paris each season to take stock of the new trends, they are messenger-doves whose mission is to indicate the probabilities of the near future. But they are neither artists nor poets. They are, above all, traders, their principal objective being to make money. Why should they introduce into America elements of novelty which would disorganise the fruits of their work, disturb the opinion of the women, who have been so skilfully trained, and compromise the success of their affairs? Thus it is that you are condemned to see nothing of the true Parisian mode except what is without personality, without significance, and with you Fashion revolves slowly, or not at all. One of these buyers once said to me, brutally:

'"I am not as interested as you are in artistic researches. The best model for me is the one I sell best. I come here for my business, and not for your art."'

'All of them think in that way, and they buy, not the most beautiful but the most banal of our models, because those will sell a greater number of copies. The effects of this method have been felt in France, where the watchword is, put a brake on the fantasy of innovators: 'Don't let us frighten the American buyers by exaggerated novelty.' And so this class of buyer, which is sought after by all the dressmaking houses, and which ought to be a vital element, does, as a matter of fact, threaten the free play of Fashion, and inevitably compromises an industry whose very raison d'être is to create novelty.

'Our houses now set out to produce variations of their last year's successes instead of inventing, and Fashion remains stationary, that is to say, anæmic, neurasthenic, and chlorotic.

'Women are dressed like a flock of school-girls as if in an institutional uniform, and that shocks me in America above all, where woman is rich and independent. Furthermore, since the War it is the American woman who has to defend the standard of luxury and elegance, for France is poor. Here women are lovely, healthy, well-balanced, blossoming like flowers, and sportive as young goddesses. How often have I not been asked what I thought of the American woman, and how often have I not replied that she is the most beautiful in the world, the most natural and most perfect type of feminine architecture, and the closest, too, to the ideal conceived by the ancient Greeks. But they lack one thing: and that is personality.'

Another time I would say to them:

'You acclaim me and I thank you for it, because I am an innovator, and because you know that I have always been in the advance guard of modern movements, even at the risk of being taken for an eccentric. But when an innovator thinks of an innovation it is at the same moment dreamed and realised, it is the miracle of flowers and fruit on a tree, a creator must not be forbidden to bear fruit, lest he should die.

'It is not always the innovator who profits from what he has invented, for a new thing ripens slowly, or rather, the public has to reflect for a long time in order to understand it. Even a modern land like America is very conservative, and if one wants to launch in it something new, it is wise to begin several years in advance, so that on the day it is launched it will no longer be new.

'When I announce to-day that short skirts have ended their reign, and when I prophesy long skirts or jupes-culotte, I produce feelings of anxiety and disquiet. The sceptics smile. I am told that I am mad. Women swear that they will never wear long skirts. They assemble to make common protest. This is like a man who refuses to buy a straw hat in June, and decides on it in September, at the moment when he will have to put it in the cupboard for the winter. This is to be perpetually behind the fashion. I am accustomed to this state of mind, and I know that you have a contradictory humour.

'When skirts were long, I had a great difficulty in getting them shortened, and to-day the short skirt, in America above all, surpasses all my most optimistic forecasts. Evidently it is the signal for a reaction. All your protests will be vain and useless. You will wear longer skirts, until the day when they will become jupes-culottes. Every kind of delaying and putting off is idle, because it is not a caprice on my part, it is the curve of evolution that decides. My prediction will be fulfilled with certainty, like that of Le Verrier, who discovered the planet Neptune and determined its dimensions long before the astronomers had been able to see it through their telescopes.

'When I suppressed petticoats in 1903, the silk manufacturers sent a deputation to me to point out that I had done an injury to their industry, and that I was yet further injuring their interests by making skirts narrower. They considered me responsible for this decision, whereas I was simply executing your desires, which I had divined before anyone else.

'Perhaps it would be better to let you believe that I command and that you have only to obey. That would be more flattering for me, but it would be less accurate. The truth is that I respond by anticipation to your secret intentions.

'There are indications which permit one to announce the end of a fashion. Very few people know how to recognise them. Thus, on the day when I announced that hats would henceforth be quite plain, it was because I had perceived that they were then covered with foliage, flowers, fruit, feathers and ribbons, and every excess in matters of fashion is a sign of the end. None the less, I received on the day following this prediction a deputation of manufacturers of flowers, fruit, foliage, feathers and ribbon who, like the Burghers of Calais, came to implore me to return to these garnishments. But what can one do against a donkey or a woman's wish? Hats remained simple, they still are; and I deplore it.

'When I announced the disappearance of stays, there was the same sensation. All the presidents of the interested Chambers of Commerce pointed out to me that I was putting on the streets a whole swarm of work-girls. I had to explain to them that women and their stays had transformed themselves throughout history, and that they would go on transforming themselves. They ought to be prepared for any eventuality.

'Finally, when I announced to the hairdressers the end of postiches, and that women would cut their hair short, they considered me as Anti-Christ. They did not take account of what would happen. Short hair is much more difficult to manage than long hair. Women don't get out of it with a permanent wave. They have to closet themselves continually with the hairdresser, whose profession has never been so prosperous.

'Thus, on each occasion, I was considered by the manufacturers as the evil tyrant who could, suddenly, with one frown, plunge a whole population into want. I am tired of playing this rôle, and so much the worse for me if it is less glorious, but I insist upon repeating to you that I am only a medium sensitive to the reactions of your taste and meticulous in registering the trends of your caprice.'

I said to the ladies of Chicago:

'Among the appellations with which it pleases people to describe me there is one which has always amused me: it is that of King of Fashion. No title is better suited to flatter a man's spirit, all the more because the King of Fashion reigns not only over one people but over all peoples, over the whole world and over sovereigns themselves. Sovereigns of states and of kingdoms, sovereigns of finance and industry, all are subject to the despotism of Fashion, which is an intolerant dictatorship. But you do not know yourselves, perhaps, to what degree you are at its mercy, for you evolve unconsciously, and you come to the point of wishing the same thing as fashion wishes, but in truth you have no free will and it is fashion which, like some astral influence, sets its impress upon you, and commands and controls your decisions, a tyrant doubly despotic since it orders women, who direct the actions of men.

'At the moment when a woman chooses or orders a dress, she believes she is doing it in all freedom, in the full exercise of her own personality, but she is deceiving herself. It is the spirit of fashion that inspires her, that reigns over her intelligence and clouds her judgment. Naturally, she defends herself against it. As you are listening to me speaking, the majority of you are thinking: 'He is exaggerating, we are not the slaves of fashion to that extent, and we know how to dispense ourselves from following it when it does not please us.'

'But here is where its miracle, its tour de force, resides; it always pleases, and its despotism is seductive by definition. Women are always of the same opinion as fashion, which changes its opinion continually.

'But who then, you will ask me, inspires this dictator's decision? No one, nor anything. It does what it wants, and wants no matter what. It has even, at every moment, a right of self-contradiction, and of taking the opposite side to the decisions it has made the day before. Everyone first grumbles, then obeys, finally applauds.

'I have heard the insinuation that the fashions of to-day are really more practical, and that women wear clothes inspired by necessity. It is the exact contrary. Fashion is endlessly illogical, and finds in its folly a satisfaction, a malicious delight. If stocks of leather become low it desires high boots, like those of airmen. If there is a lack of sable, that is the fur fashion seeks out. It desires only that which is rare, because that which is rare is dear.

'The spirit of contradiction in Fashion is so frequent and so regular that one can see in it almost a law. Do not women wear fox furs on light dresses, velvet hats in August, and straw ones in February? It was in the period of narrow Sedan chairs that they clothed themselves in the most abundant and encumbering paniers. It was in the period of uncomfortable diligences that they wore crinolines – and one must add this spicy detail, which shows that they knew their error, the crinolines could be deflated at will. They were supported by three or four rows of steel springs that were inserted into slips. When they got into a carriage these springs were taken out and rolled up into a small space, and put into a box. On arrival at her destination, the lady fled into the first room she could find in the inn, hurriedly re-inserted the springs into the slips and appeared in the courtyard of the hostelry stiff and spruce as the corolla of a flower.

'There is in the decisions of fashion and of women a kind of provocation to common sense that is charming, and that can only annoy soured souls.

'A few years ago, all summer hats had large brims. This was reasonable, since they were intended to protect against the rays of the sun; they could not last. To-day, they have, so to say, no brims at all; at the same time, ladies showed their hair and when they did not have enough they sewed postiches on to the brim of the hat. No one then would have dared to hide the nape of her neck, her cranium and her forehead in a toque rammed right down over the eyebrows. Fashion was intolerant then; it still is; but in the opposite direction.

'Similarly, was there one woman, who, fifty years ago, could have worn pink or beige stockings like those you wear to-day? All stockings were compulsorily black, just as, in 1840, they were white. In the period of white stockings you would not have dared risk a pair of black ones; in the period of black stockings you would not have found a single pair of pink in the shops, and to-day – go and look for black ones!

'"What will they be to-morrow?" I was asked by a journalist.

'"I see no reason," I replied to him, "why there may not be worn a stocking of one colour on one leg, and of another on the other. You laugh? But that has already happened, and in the period when it was the turn of black you would not have dared to put on white."

'Consequently, and that is the point I want to make, you must not cry out that something not admitted to-day is a scandal. For it will be accepted to-morrow. In matters of fashion there is never anything *likely*; all is excess, and convention.

'If to-morrow in Fifth Avenue you saw an elegant woman wearing a bustle you would be astounded, or if she wore the garment that will be yours in twenty years' time, you would refuse to believe it, for in every period everybody firmly believes that the fashion of the moment is the definitive, the most reasonable and most æsthetic form. It is nothing of the sort, and one must always expect the unforeseen, on the contrary, and when one predicts fashion, one must not fear to go far, and audaciously. For fashion always surpasses prognostication. So, why resist its suggestions, why protest against the jupe-culotte? It is coming irresistibly. It has entered in amongst us in the form of pyjamas. Did not your grandmothers cry out when they saw you adopt this masculine toilette, even for night wear? To-day you wear it for lunch, and you have variants on the same theme for dinner. It was already worn in Paris several years ago. It needed the clumsiness of a Bechoff, who wanted to win notoriety for himself by having them worn at the races, to make the first attempt fail. But the jupe-culotte is ineluctable, and I believe that America is on the point of adopting its liberating formula, which will open up possibilities for the invention of creators, whereas the present fashion for skirts stumbles along repetitively.'

And I said to the dames of Los Angeles:

'When hundreds of lovely women are gathered together in the same hall, because of an interest in Fashion, one may well ask oneself what rôle can a man play in such a matter? Do you really believe that a man can teach anything to you in matters of elegance? There is something ridiculous about attempting it, and he who comes to instruct you asks himself, to-day as he looks at you, if it is not he who is about to receive a lesson.

'For I have crossed the Atlantic to speak to you of Fashion. A Frenchman, as you know, does not like travelling. A Frenchman loves his own home, he is faithful to his accustomed habits, attached to his family, and he finds his pleasure within a narrow frame. He is like a bird who loves his cage and who, when the door is opened, refuses to depart from it. And let us admit that there are sound reasons to keep him at home. Beside his wife, who is by definition charming, there is cooking, the pleasures of the table and . . . wines which cannot be found everywhere. I, who am French and very appreciative of the charms of wine, understand very well why one hesitates to leave one's own country. And yet, America attracts me irresistibly. I have already been here twice before, and it seems to me that I have need of its atmosphere of activity and of its practical spirit, of its clarity, its intelligence and sense of work. All young Frenchmen ought to come to America at least once, and all the old ones even more so.

'To-day, I have come to preach a crusade to you. I want to cry out to the women of America: "Take care! You are being deceived. You imagine you are being provided with the fashions of Paris; but you do not see them! You send to Paris emissaries commissioned to inform you, but they do not tell you what they see. You are women who have won your freedom, cinema 'stars,' rich, liberated, independent. Come to Paris!"

'When you go into an American house, they sell you a model, it is a 42 or a 44 or a 46. You are catalogued according to your dimensions, you are a number. In Paris you will have the impression that a special model is being made for you, taking account of your own personality, your character, and your habits.

'Visit the great dressmakers, and you will not feel that you are in a shop, but in the studio of an artist, who intends to make of your dresses a portrait and a likeness of yourself. As soon as you have passed the wrought-iron gates, you will come first upon an archaic bust of an ancient Venus. It is set up in the entrance hall, as if in homage to all the graces and all the splendours of woman. Then you will ascend to the first floor, by a marble staircase, where you will find bronze deer, whose origin is Herculanum. They symbolize elegance.

'Then, you will enter upon vast salons tapestried in rose and silver like the grottoes of the nymphs of Calypso. If you are truly a woman, you will be unable not to lose your head when you see the mirrors, the lights, the soft colours – and your sensitivity will be softened, ready to receive the strong impressions that are awaiting you.

'Here are models that come with majestic grace, like divinities whose feet touch not the ground. There is no noise, no booming organ, no gramophone. This is a Temple of Beauty, and you will have to summon to your aid all the wisdom and all the subtlety of woman to avoid sinking beneath the temptations that harass you. A *vendeuse* is standing behind you, she controls your ravishment. If you are strong, there is still time to get up, and depart, saying that you will come back again in a day or two. But if you are a woman, you will not be able to say that you do not desire to wear at least one of these marvels, that contain all the admiration, all the tenderness, all the love, for let us speak the word, which an artist can express by means of stuffs.

'Am I a fool when I dream of putting art into my dresses, a fool when I say that dressmaking is an art?'

At Chickasha, in Oklahoma, I spoke to 3,000 girls, and I said to them: 'It is not from fashion journals that you will learn how to be beautiful. What have you got to do with fashion? So, don't bother yourself with it, and simply wear what becomes you. Look at yourselves in the mirror. Observe those tones that enhance the brilliance of your own colours, and those that dim them. Adopt those which are favourable to you, and if blue suits you, don't think you ought to wear green because green is the fashion.'

After I had developed this theme for an hour, I asked my audience if anyone had a question to ask.

Little folded papers were passed up to me, on which were written the following questions:

'What will be the fashionable nuance this winter?'

Or:

'What colour should one wear for a wedding?'

They had understood nothing, or perhaps heard nothing.

To repair this mishap, the girls' Directress gave permission to the pupils of the senior classes to parade past me in order to learn from my own mouth which was the colour that each ought to adopt. Thus, I saw file by in front of me 1,500 virgins, into whose eyes I stared to discover the colour of their irises, and I had to say immediately, like a seer, the tone that suited them. I said: 'Blue, green, garnet,' and the young ladies withdrew content.

You must know that I was fee'd a thousand dollars a lecture. You will agree that it was not too much.

When I say that I was fee'd I am speaking the exact truth, for my manager became undiscoverable at the moment when our accounts had to be settled. He owed me a quarter of a million francs; I looked for him everywhere, in his own home and elsewhere, and I had to quit America leaving my lawyer to pursue him. It was a delicate mission, for he was fond of aviation, and you will have read in the newspapers that he killed himself when he tried to land on the roof of a building. He left nothing but children and debts.

I have turned up some notes I wrote in the course of my first journeys when I was under the influence of strong new impressions. Here they are:

How can one look upon that heaped up pile of architecture that is New York, seen from the Hudson, without being constricted, as if one had been seized by the hand of a giant? From the instant when one has first set eyes on this prodigious ensemble, one admires, and one is overwhelmed.

It is from this very overwhelming that a great deal of criticism arises. There is a discrepancy of scale between the American dimensions and those of the little man in the street from anywhere and everywhere, who comes to see them. He cannot adapt himself instantaneously, and he feels a certain uneasiness and suffers without knowing from what cause.

America? A great many floors, or at any rate, a great many lifts, a great many pairs of spectacles, a great deal of iced water, but not the least whim or fancy.

The street is full of men and women, not one curious glance, not one ogle. They do not know what there can be of sympathy, or reserve, or desire, or respect, in an eye glance. Here, eyes have no expression. They look. Do they see?

One evening, returning from the theatre, I stopped to gaze upon a fairy landscape. I was on a broad pavement. Large and comfortable cars rolled noiselessly past me. They were like shadows, like spectral carriages, and in front of me, at a prodigious height, I saw the profiles of the buildings, implacable blocks perforated with regular windows. Into the sky there climbed belfries, belvederes, temples, frontons, lit up by a rose light so that one could have thought them suspended, hung from the stars. On every side towers and spires and cathedrals sprang towards the black velvet of the sky, some illuminated from top to bottom, others dark, but bearing on their summits a golden flame.

What beings, what forces, what gods could inhabit these edifices? I pondered, and as I started to walk again, I perceived new belfries, an immensity of superposed cubes, massed dream castles, keeps and ramparts over which played light and shade. I stood as overwhelmed as after hearing those symphonies that make one's arteries pulsate, and dilate the heart almost to paroxysm. It was New York that was before me, and instantly I had a clear conception of its force.

What can one compare to this spectacle? Perhaps the civilisation of ancient Rome. What difference is there between a gladiator in the Colosseum at Rome, and the combat between Tunney and Dempsey, beneath the eyes of 50,000 spectators, or the Army-Princeton match? The same humanity is moved by the same passions, and still believes in progress. It evolves ceaselessly and always comes back to its starting point, and despite constant effort, and spiritual victories and scientific discoveries, and miracles of daring, it remains subject to the same desires and a slave to the same passions.

As I dictate this chapter I have before my eyes the letters I wrote from Harrisburg, Pennsylvania, and Minneapolis, Minnesota. I had changed my train in Chicago, and between the two stations I had been taken in an automobile at a vertiginous pace. I had seen the great Avenue along which I, with a torrent of other cars, was rolling, suddenly raise itself perpendicularly – in an instant the cars put on their brakes, forming a queue. The road and the pavement became a wall in front of us. For a few moments they remained vertical, a ship was passing: then they sank down again with the same regular and rapid movement. The traffic, for a moment suspended, resumed its course. The stop, the manœuvring of the bridge, the resumption, all passed in silence, not a Klaxon, nor any impatience or agitation, not a word. At the station, a negro seized my luggage and took the number of my place in the train, assuring me that I should find him there. Should I?

A rapid déjeuner, or rather, a quick lunch, Blue-Points, Cassaba-melon; I glance at the papers: 'Armed bandits are terrorising Chicago and defying the police with admirable ingenuity.' The station platform, on each side a train de luxe, stretches like a narrow street between black houses whose windows sparkle. Crowds stream out in silence. Plumes of smoke. The sound of bells. Luggage. I think I have seen this in *Round the World in 24 Days*. Then the street becomes alive, the travellers, sagely, like conscious automata, give up their tickets to the negroes who, in their black liveries, meticulously polished, appetizing, are on duty outside each carriage. They receive with smiles their grave and preoccupied guests. No relatives, no old friends, encumber the platform-lane. But no, here is a noble mother, covered with furs, trimmed with monkey, her mouth tight, accompanying her daughter, who is about to depart. There are no words, no vociferations, but two real tears suddenly outline her cheeks. Am I really in America? I could think myself at the Châtelet. And here comes the little multi-millionairess in her grey astrakhan cloak with snowboots to her knees and a bouquet of red cherries pinned to her collar. All get into the train, I find by my seat my luggage and my negro, grinning from ear to ear. A tip. A whistle. We have started. Without noise or jerk we are going 55 miles an hour without seeming to move.

I make an inspection of my apartments. Here is the dining room, with the negro servants clothed and gloved in white. In the Club-car, a compartment in dark mahogany (mahogany coloured, but it is composed of steel), which is reserved for men, there are two rows of deep armchairs, in which I can perceive nothing save spectacles, newspapers and cigars. Faces manufactured by mass production, and standardised so highly that I could not recognise them apart. They all have the same fixed and obstinate expression.

We pass through snow-covered country, flat and desolate steppes, then agglomerations of bungalows divided by avenues, along which there gallop amazons riding astride, jockey caps on their heads, their red hair blown in the wind.

Further on there are groups of gigantic factories, like barracks or roofless châteaux. Their high chimneys have on them immense vertical letters, telling the nature of their productions: 'Hobart Fine Pianos,'

```
A        E
M    F   Q
E    O   U
R    U   I
I    N   P
C    D   M
A    R   E
N    Y   N
         T
```

Smoking publicity!

An official, tastefully gold braided, asks me my name, in case a telegram should arrive for me en route. He shows me his own compartment, where his staff is ready to take down my dictation. I cannot resist taking advantage of these luxurious facilities. I shall telegraph to no matter which of my friends, for fun, but I would very much like to receive a telegram, and I know that I shall not have one. A pity.

Everywhere are conveniences of which I cannot make use. Spittoons. I do not spit.

Writing desks. I do not write on trains. Wells in the tables for bottles and glasses. But nothing is drunk here but mineral waters.

In the middle of the carriage an aged gentleman, bald and very distinguished, who looks as if he had never been in a temper in his life, smokes a cigar even longer than my own, which cost me eighteen francs. At his side an aged secretary listens to him and takes down notes. He gives out a dulled sound, as if he were a thinking rattle. It is impossible to understand what he is saying. He is very serious. He never smiles. Nobody, in any case, dreams of smiling. It is very long since I have seen a smile. Are they all, then, in France? Here there are only grins. People don't come here to make merry. What is a country where they smile all the time? Is it not only an amusement place, fit to pass a holiday?

I return to my seat, and discover on it a little printed notice which tells me of the innovations which have been applied to this model train, which is called the 'Twentieth Century Limited'; this train by itself represents a capital of $1,460,000, I am informed. I am glad to know it, but it is not very delicate to tell me.

It requires thirty-two employees, without counting the barber, who has his own shop, nor the valet in his, who presses suits during the night, nor the certificated nurse put at the service of the women and children, with her own apartment in which she can give baths, and also manicure treatment. Then, finally, there is an observation car; this is a covered platform placed at the end of the train ending in a balcony whence one can enjoy the landscape, seated in a comfortable garden chair. But . . . there is no landscape.

XIX
Gastronomy

I said at the beginning of this book that when I was a child I had no appetite. I owe it to truth to admit that with increasing age I have become a gourmand, and some of my friends insist that to-day I am to be considered a connoisseur in matters of gastronomy. It is an empirical science, in which all the world can participate in France, where there are both the best foodstuffs, and the most skilled cooks.

To be a gourmet – that requires a special education, composed of many fortunate or unfortunate experiments. It requires crusades into the Bordeaux country, expeditions into Champagne and Burgundy, to appreciate there in their own district, the ranged vintages, and to practise the faculties of one's palate.

In an hotel at Epernay I once saw some foreigners asking for Sauterne. Was that not heretical?

I have seen the head waiter of 'La Tour d'Argent,' that conservatory of gastronomic tradition, weep because foreigners were emptying his cellar without appreciating it. 'They are infidels,' he said to me, 'who buy my rarest specimens, my Lur-Saluces '63, my Château-Laffitte '75, my Haut-Brion 1900, and at the end of their meal ask me for a glass of beer, because they are still thirsty! The great connoisseurs are dying out, and our fine wines also. How can we reconstitute the wine libraries and œnological museums of a Braquessac, of the Café Voisin, or of the Maison Dorée, or the Café Anglais?'

For my part, I consider that an artist should only eat good things, and should flee from ill food as much as from ill sights. I prefer to go without dinner, rather than eat an unwholesome or unappetising meal. The ordering and preparation of a pleasant dinner has always seemed to me an occupation worthy of an aristocrat.

Cooking, like smoke, can rise above the kitchen range, and one can find spiritual satisfaction both in doing and in eating it. That, at least, is what I think, every time I lunch with my friend Verdier, a great chef of the old school, who has written the most enlightened cookery books.

I was a member of an association of gourmets which was called 'Le Club des Cents': this club caused me vexations which I think I ought to recount now, in order to dissipate persistent gossip.

The president of this association, which existed to assemble one hundred friends all more or less gourmets, was one Nathan, called Louis Forest. He was a journalist, and he suffered from stomach trouble. When he presided over a banquet he would take from his pocket two new laid eggs which he discreetly gave to the cook with the prescription 'three minutes.' Thus, his function was purely honorific and did not oblige him, as you will agree, to contract gastritis.

One day we were convoked to a dinner of the club at 'La Peniche Parisienne,' which, before the Battle of the Marne, had been the property and the home of Marshal Joffre. The invitation stipulated that no guests should be brought. It was to be only members of the Club.

We sat down to dinner. I had beside me my friend Creste, and on the other side my friend Lamberjack, a former champion cyclist of the great days, who had a free tongue in his head and sometimes made lightning repartees. That, in any case, was part of his charm.

I will say with La Fontaine:

> *The banquet was very excellent;*
> *Nothing lacked at the feast.*
> *But someone disturbed the party.*

Towards the end of the repast a gentleman whom I did not know, and who had not been introduced to us, stood up at the president's side to boast the charms and sing the praises of a wine he wanted us to sample. He had brought fifty bottles of it. It was a Château de —— which seemed to me an unspeakable drink. (I won't give its name, first of all because I don't want to be prosecuted, and secondly because it does not deserve mention by me.) This wine, so said this representative of commerce, was manufactured according to the purest traditions of Touraine, and he was going to spread himself in divagations on his theme when he was stopped by the protests of

Lamberjack and myself: our official reunions should not be used for the purpose of advertising commercial brands, and this was laid down in our rules.

The gentleman was requested to sit down, and our observations were supported by a general approving murmur. But M. de —— insisted on going on, saying that he had no intention of advertisement and that his wine was sufficiently well known to do without it, but he simply wished to demonstrate to us that it was obtained by secular practice and procedures, that had nowadays disappeared from Touraine, and that it had every guarantee of good manufacture, etc., etc., so that I rose from my place and cried:

'Enough of that! Have you got your order book with you! Write me down for 200 bottles, and sit down!'

It seems that this interjection caused a chill, that M. de —— was the personal guest of the president. (Ah ha, but I thought that there were no guests!) My friends gathered round me to show me their solidarity in my support, and I departed.

The very next day I sent to the president Nathan, called Louis Forest, my resignation as a member of the Club.

I received no acknowledgment of the letter, but I was requested to appear before a disciplinary committee. I replied to him that I would not lend myself to this kind of jurisdiction, and I again offered my resignation. Following upon this letter, the Committee, or the Council, functioning as a tribunal of honour, pronounced my expulsion.

A little while after there was another meeting, to which, naturally, I was not invited. Most of my friends took part, the events of the preceding session were recounted, and travestied by the president. There must have been acid comments and wrangling. In consequence of this dinner my friends assembled about me and founded a new group, which was called in derision, 'Le Club des Pur-Cents,' and I was asked to accept its presidency, for I had been the reason for its constitution. The two clubs still exist, and continue their rival activities . . .

Since that day I have had many good dinners, without ever touching the Château de ——

I have been drawn to carry out certain recipes myself, and to create specialities of my own. I make an omelette stuffed with shallots and chives, which I consider a little marvel. But without contradiction, my triumph is *l'œuf du pêcheur*, whose recipe I want to tell you.

When you eat mussels, keep the juice. I have always liked to supervise and control the deeds and works of my cooks, of whom the most famous were, beyond a doubt, Aurélie and Catherine. I certainly owe them this honourable mention in return for all the joys they gave me. From them I learned *tourne-mains* whose secret I guard piously, and my heart is as full of gratitude as my belly.

I dictate these lines seated in my kitchen garden, among my beans and tomatoes, and upon these I gaze not without pleasure, thinking of the delights they promise me. As this book goes to America, I shall be thought very puerile to attach so much importance to these fresh vegetables which, over there, are industrial productions that come to the housewife in tins, which I denounce; for if tomatoes are creations of God, tins are an invention of men.

I can never think without terror of all the good cooks America has taken from us and who have become, in the laboratories of its great hotels, alchemists and chemical calculators . . . I would like to be rich enough to be able to do something for French cookery, and save its traditions, which are being compromised by the number of foreigners who live in Paris in absolute ignorance of culinary tradition. They entice with their dollars all our cordons-bleus, and know not what to ask of them, showing the same appetite for a tabloid soup as for a true and loyal *garbure* that retains all its natural tastes and colours; where the cabbage is green, the carrot red, the turnip white, and the bacon pink, and the peas fresh and free from bicarbonate of soda.

I hope to retain to the end of my days a sufficient appetite to appreciate cooking, which is for me a *violon d'Ingres*.

For the *violon d'Ingres* is often spoken of, and in France all the Ingres have their violons. But for me a violin is a small thing, I have wanted to have an oboe, a clarionet, and to ask from all the arts the satisfactions they can give. And for this a great many people have reproached me.

I sought in dramatic art a diversion from my customary occupations, and I accepted an offer from Colette, which led me onto the stage. I should never have believed that the theatre was still considered a degrading profession. In the time of Molière, actors were deprived of proper burial, and one would say that something remains of the traditions to-day. I can still hear the voice of M. Lazare Weiler, a senator and president of my Board of Directors, pointing out to me the incongruity of my appearing on a Parisian stage, even as an amateur. For my part, since for me the greatest luxury of life has always been to be independent, and do what pleased me, I am unable to make myself regret that period when I was very excellently amused throughout a provincial tour, in the company of that great writer who is Colette, and her interpreters: and then for a month in Paris, when every evening I put on the appearance of a personage new to me.

And from books, too, I asked that they should give me divers delights, not only from the literature they contained, but by the refinements of their appearance. At the time when I was working with Dufy, we had undertaken and established an Annual, which I had called 'L'Almanach des Lettres et des Arts.' It was printed on fine paper, and illustrated with woodcuts by Dufy, and it bore the names of all the pioneer artists and writers. I also had to my credit Iribe's Album and that of Lepape, of which I have already spoken. I was further to produce a cookery book in which I gathered together recipes culled from the best sources: the great amateurs and the great chefs who were my friends. I had the book illustrated in piquant fashion by a lady gourmande, full of sensitivity, who is called Marie-Alix.

I produced yet another book, of so quite special a quality that I scarcely dare speak of it; it was called 'Popolôrepô: pages chosen by one fool and illustrated by another.' The other was Pierre Fau, who had as much malice as the first. In this book one reads things of this sort:

'*Ma riche amie Marie n'a ni ami ni mari. Vous savez sa vie: son père marin mort à Marmara, sa mère remariée est Maharanie de Caramanie. Son parrain est à Marennes, sa Marraine est à Parie. N'enviez pas sa vie.*'

I am embarrassed at having had to give an extract and specimen of these divagations, but since I have shown you the nature of my activities, I must also give you an idea of my diversions. At least I have the excuse of not taking seriously these depravities, and not pretending to make them the basis of a new poetry.

Secretions of thought in this kind have, in any case, been ennobled and enriched by the example of a few geniuses: Victor Hugo, Théophile Gautier, etc.

The last book I published was an advertising album that attracted great attention: the Annual *Pan*. It addressed itself to every luxury trade and industry; it had been created in joy, like all good things, and it had been the occasion for a weekly reunion of all the best designers of the period, who lunched with me on Wednesdays. To each was entrusted a particular problem of publicity: for instance, he had to laud in some unforeseen, telling way the unique beads of Clause, the suits of the tailor O'Rossen, or the precious finds of the antiquary Bensimon.

Martin, Dignimont, Touchagues, Lucien Boucher, Oberlé, Camille Bellaigue, Pierre Fau, Eddy Legrand, Piaubert, Georges Delaw, and Van Moppés, and the animal designer, Delhuermoz, were my faithful habitués. Some of them, who were not yet known, found their opportunity in this work. The album *Pan* circulated not only amongst the clientèle it aimed at, but all the amateurs of art and bib-liophiles demanded a copy. One day it will be exhumed, and will become the model for a new magazine.

At that period I began, with the assistance of the same artists, to establish a collection of illustrated books, of which there was only one copy each. I would choose, for instance, a book by Jules Renard, printed on fine paper, like the Bernouard edition, and I would give it to one of my designers to read, to whichever seemed to me to have a temperament sympathetic to that of the writer, Georges Delaw in this case, and I would authorise him to make, in the course of his reading, sketches, water-colours and comments, in the margins, or even on the pages. I had to suspend the formation of this collection, and stop the expenditure in which it involved me. But I very much hope to resume it, one day, and go very far with it.

It will console me for my loss on the day I was forced by financial calamities to disperse the pictures I had so ardently collected. But is it not the destiny of every collector that he should accumulate a cer-tain number of charming masterpieces, to see them one day dispersed at the chance of the auction room, and re-grouped according to other patterns? I do not feel the least bit in the world Bolshevist, but I consider that an individual has no right to seize for himself works of art, which constitute the national patrimony, simply because he is rich. He who has the means to collect pictures should also provide a livelihood for artists, and should be obliged, periodically, to submit his acquisitions to the public, by giving an exhibition in some State gallery. He should be authorised to compound for this obligation by paying a sum to be employed for the purchase of works by artists not yet famous. This idea I suggest, in passing, for any enterprising minister who wants to do something useful and new.

If the *objets d'art* and the books I have collected were to be examined, a great many people would be astonished to find nothing outrageous among them. Few or no Cubists, and not the slightest Surrealism. I cannot support an artistic language that speaks in a nebulous and inaccessible idiom. Nature seems to me to express herself clearly; why, therefore, should man seek to complicate it? That perhaps was what Jean Cocteau wanted to say to me on a Sunday afternoon when he visited me – I had stayed in bed after a tumultuous Saturday. He came into my room and said that I had remained a simple garden flower and he added:

'You are right, my dear Poiret, . . . everyone will have to come back to simplicity . . . we shall all come back to it one of these days.'

And I thought that this was what he was trying to do, too late, perhaps.

And yet, is there any other procedure for a creator, than to assuage his thirst exclusively from the living springs of nature, and give her back generously what he has borrowed? All who strive to find outside nature the origin of their inspiration are in danger of sophistication, or extravagance. Poison can only give rise to monstrosities, deformities, gibbosities; while nature, on the contrary, whose enticement is at once stimulating and satisfying, dispenses only harmony and measure. It has always been my principle not to impair my physical or moral health, which is the very condition of my continual good humour and delight in work. The whole secret is there. If I am doing cooking or if I am making an evening gown, I give myself wholly to it, merrily, and I feel no constraint. I bring the same taste, the same care and the same goodwill to all my occupations, and I give myself wholly to each of my works.

I hope this can be seen, and that, when anyone looks at one of my creations he can see in it the feeling and the sparkle that went out from me. It is probably this that has tempted those who have tried to copy my enterprises for themselves. Unhappily for them, they have not understood the necessity of respecting my ways, my habitual methods. They have not known the right way to go about it.

On my return from a visit to America, I perceived that a beast of prey had visited my nest. The shark had carried off four of my chief employees, and he thought that thereby he held something of me. He thought that with them he was taking away sufficient elements to be able to reconstitute my House without me, but how should the cuckoo know how to bring up the little ones he has stolen? He does not brood the eggs, he breaks them and he eats them. What has become of the unhappy wretches he stole from me? They are to-day dispersed and objectless, because they are without the flame I knew how to communicate to them, and which came forth from my heart and my thoughts. How could they not have foreseen this? What presumption blinded them?

Everything I have created I have done from out myself, urged by a personal intuition, and desire, and I have achieved the final realisation without recourse to anyone. Doubtless I was surrounded by employees and collaborators, but it was I who inspired them, and none of them has done anything since leaving me. I have not known one who succeeded in getting himself talked about, or imposing himself upon the public.

An artist encloses himself in his work, he projects something of himself into everything he undertakes, and he presents himself wholly in each of his creations. By a phenomenon which must be a kind of radio-activity he divides himself, I think, at the impulse of his will, and he passes into his work in potentiality, and perhaps in substance: that is what makes us so greatly moved when we look at the paintings of certain masters, for they reveal the effective presence of the author. What sensitive person has not felt this before the works of Giotto, El Greco, Vermeer, or Chardin?

Doubtless the miracle does not always take place, but when circumstances are propitious and inspiration rich and full, this sort of transfusion is produced, and if my belief has any foundation, I hope that my presence has been recognised in many of my works, because of the amount of passion and the strength of love I have expended in their creation.

Whatever the nature of the enterprise, and whatever the domain of my activities, I have put into everything I have done my whole personality and my whole sensibility.

If Cocteau had seen me this morning he would truly have said that I was a simple flower. He would have found me in my kitchen, whose windows open upon a noisy poultry yard; I was preparing a *dorade grillée au beurre blanc*, and a *pintade aux choux* for the entertainment of a friend. I refuse to consider this as either low or naïf, but I take it as a proof of strength and independence, and I am very far from blushing for it. Who can give an idea of that unique and pure satisfaction that is savoured by the creator before his realised ideal? How many things have I not brought into the world, with that feeling of plenitude which is the recompense of effort?

I wanted to draw from the leaves of certain plants perfumes that till then had only been sought from the flowers and the roots. I amused myself by working upon the leaf of the geranium, from which I made the perfume I called Borgia, then upon mastic and the balsamic plants of the Provençal heaths. I went to the glass-blowers, to execute my models for the flasks and flagons to enclose these essences. I had my glassware decorated by pupils of my School of Decorative Art, who illumined them with charming flowers and arabesques. At the same time, I had tapestries woven and printed which no one before me had dreamed of. I went to Venice where I gave the artists of Murano designs for lustres which they blew under my eyes, and I saw my models come forth from their magic rods. I went to Milan to choose brocades inspired by the treasures of cathedrals. I had made specially for me, by the weavers of Lyons, wholly new designs; I have guided the hands of the artists who covered with reliefs the walls of the palaces of my time.

> . . . *J'ai donné des avis aux ouvriers du Nonce*
> *Occupés à sculpter sur la porte un Bacchus* . . .

And I created new shapes which were sometimes sheaths and dalmatics; sometimes corollas and bells. I gave them form, colour, movement and life. I gave them also a world-wide reputation, and the respect of the public. It was too much. There came bankers who wanted to canalise it all, who seized hold over all my activities, and thought they could master them. Then it was as if a doctor, wishing to treat by force a healthy man, had compressed his lungs and applied a pneumo-thorax apparatus, – the artificial replacing the natural.

'What is the good of all this useless caprice? Perfumes from leaves? Tell me of a good shaving cream, find for me, you who claim to be an artist, a name by which I may baptise the product in this tube – which allays all chafing of the skin. Your flasks and all your new ideas, we don't want them, they cost too much. We are bankers, and not artists, we want to make money! Enough and too much of your eccentricities, we must have everyday things that can be sold to all the world; we work by method, we do, and we don't fling about our money.'

Another said to me: 'Your jupe-culotte is a piece of imbecility. We don't want it, it irritates the clientèle, you have made ridiculous models, and we cannot show them, and since you cannot understand us, we shall not go on paying you. Ah! Ah! Ah!'

And a third forbade me to carry out any new designs in furnishings or tapestries. 'We must first sell,' he said, 'everything we have in stock.' I could no longer approach the manufacturers, nor inspire anyone. The staff had received orders to cease all contact with me. Imagine all the witches and wicked fairies gathered together by the Queen's bedside, to prevent her from being delivered. She could not but die.

But lo! the Queen has disappeared, and the wicked fairies have perished. Ah! Ah! Ah!

XX
The Philosopher

So, here it is, whole and entire, this life that has lasted fifty years. It has gone into a volume of three hundred and thirty-one pages. Should it have been filled out? I am not sorry to have looked at it as a whole, and to consider it to-day in foreshortened perspective. I have probably had more pleasure than my readers in this labour.

I have tried to follow the progression of the arabesque which, it seems to me, has developed pretty regularly since my birth, like those ribbons which magicians wind around a stick and which, following more and more eccentric orbs and spirals, give an effect of spreading out into immense flower figures. I have been the hearth of many things, or rather, I should say, the fire that has lit up many hearths; but these hearths have gone out or become choked with ash, as they have departed from me. I have never seen a success made by anyone who has betrayed me. It seems to me that I have lived through a fine adventure, and I still enjoy the consideration of all its phases, even including that fête of the 24th of December, 1924, when all the asses had given one another rendezvous at my house without being invited. I found myself hemmed in by a black band, one of those worldly and distinguished bands called a consortium. Fur cloaks were missing from the vestibule. I was asked for a great many which had never existed. J. L. F., who had none in coming, departed by mistake with a comfortable pelisse. Mme M—— S—— discovered, as she was going out, her otter cloak on the shoulders of a lady who had never been invited. It was the end of everything.

A few days later I was turned into a limited company. Everyone knows the rest of the story.

When a pedestrian is found seated in the early morning at the edge of the pavement, his eye haggard and his face bruised, the kindly policeman who questions him asks him to relate in detail what happened to him; he replies:

'I cannot remember. I know that they were numerous. There was one who struck. The others kept watch. I am not sure that I could recognise them again, except two or three . . . but one of these days the police . . . for they are professionals.'

I am in exactly the same position. I bear no resentment. I have accustomed myself to being no longer rich. He who has not got used to it is my tax collector. There are people who continue to demand money from me as if it were only natural that I should have it. I am surprised that one can be so happy without it. I live in a pretty countryside in the *Ile de France*, and if sometimes there is gloom within my room, my window opens vastly upon a superb view, and lets air and light, and the heat of the sun, and the freshness of night, enter in freely. I am alone (yes, dear lady, quite alone), although I still have some friends, and I have children whom I adore, and who I think love me, although I often scold them, because I would like them to know all that I know.

I have resumed with passionate devotion painting, which I have always loved and never forsook; and nothing seems to me better nor more beautiful than to express in colours, as if they were primal cries, all the emotion that is caused in one by the contemplation of nature. People have said that it was not I who painted my pictures. Certainly, too, there will one day appear some idiot who will say that this book was written by another.

It has been suggested to me that I should return to business activities. That may well happen. I feel I have many dresses within me. In that case I will perhaps, some day, write a second volume of memoirs. But I must beg the reader to excuse me if, because of a circumstance independent of my will, it should be less thick than this one.